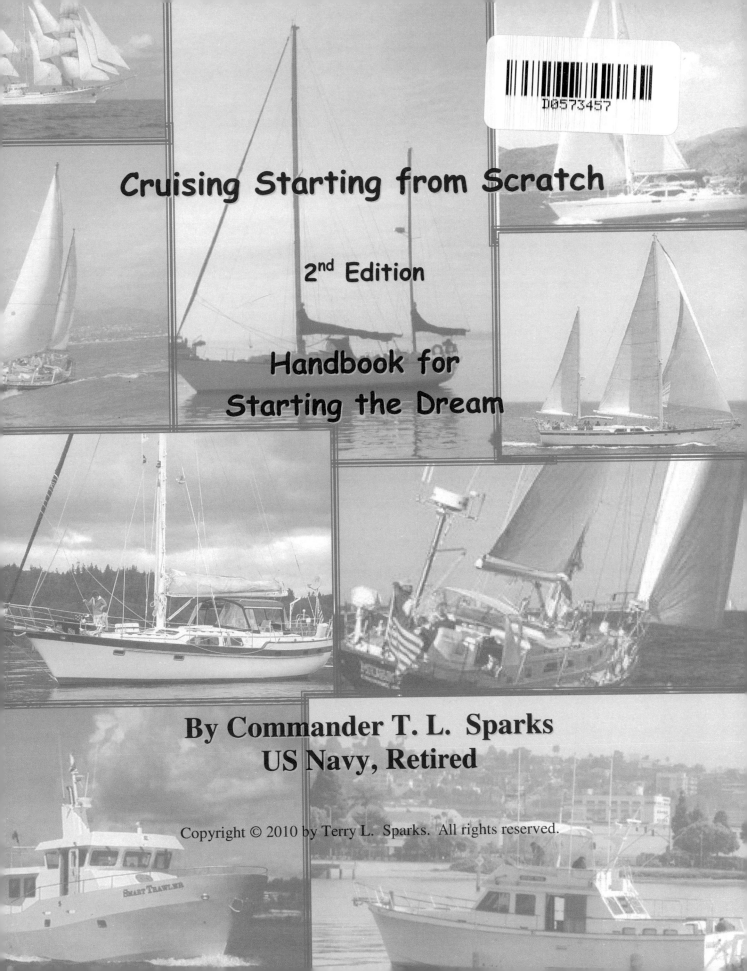

Cruising Starting from Scratch

2nd Edition

Handbook for Starting the Dream

By Commander T. L. Sparks
US Navy, Retired

Foreword – Creating the Dream

Fifteen years ago my wife Pat and I were in the Caribbean and came to the realization that we wanted to retire down in the Caribbean on a sailboat. We wanted to live the carefree life. If that sounds like something you have been thinking about and maybe even planning, then this book might be for you. The book is not a detailed education on sailing, but an overview of all aspects that must be considered in the planning process. While you may be able to find several books on cruising, this book will be a helpful tool to transport you from the conceptual idea of a sailing retirement to the reality of doing it.

I served almost 34 years in the US Navy and Naval Reserve. Even with that career background there were a lot of things to learn about cruising in a sailboat. I collected a significant amount of information, as I worked through the five year planning and training to prepare for cruising life.

A joke I heard one time really sets the stage for this book. *Two guys in a bar and one asked the other: What is the difference in a Power Boater and a Sailboat Cruiser?*

His friend explained: A Sailor has to know his/her boat, learn navigation, use of radar, use GPS, learn celestial navigation, learn to read charts, learn to repair the engine and other systems on the boat, learn to maintain and repair the sails, learn to tie knots, etc, etc, etc, etc.

A Power Boater just needs to have lots of money, a gold chain and a case of beer. If they do not have enough money to buy the boat, they at least need to have good credit.

While frequently many power boaters know a lot more than some sailors, it should be clear that with respect to sailors, and especially cruising sailors, the list of skills that a cruiser must attain to be successful and safe is long. This book covers each subject in enough detail that you will begin to understand the magnitude of what you don't know.

Files to include spreadsheets and other information to help individuals through the process are available for this book by sending an email to me at: p-t_on_sunyside@live.com. Be sure and put (files for "Starting from Scratch") in the subject line so I open the email.

Note: The first addition of this book was only available on CD from me directly.

About the author

I retired from the Naval Reserve as a full Commander. My Naval career started as an electronics technician repairing communications, radar, computer and satellite tracking equipment. I stood watches in navigation, radar and sonar. After leaving active duty I went back to school and attained a Bachelor of Science degree in Electrical Engineering. At the 15 year point in my Navy Reserve career, I was promoted to Ensign. Ultimately I was promoted to Commander and a few years later I retired from the Naval Reserve.

Civilian positions have included Chief Engineer at a television station, teaching electronics at a community college, systems engineer and engineering and software development management. I retired from ABB Inc., one of the world's largest Electrical Engineering companies, in 2008

I had sailed on 20-35 foot power and sailboats until September 2000 when my wife Pat and I purchased a 45 foot sailboat named Sunnyside. For ten years, Pat and I have prepared the boat for retirement and cruising. Summer vacations were test runs for enjoyment as well as understanding vulnerabilities that needed to be resolved before heading across an ocean. At the end of the first cruise from Portland to Puget Sound, the upgrade list was several pages. As the boat was refined for cruising, the list became very short and finally went away.

Since the information needed to make sure the boat was ready to go was attained from many books, web pages, and friends, I decided to consolidate the information into this book to make it simpler for others to get started to live the dream cruising.

You can also follow our cruising adventure at our web page and find out where we are today at: http://sunnyside-adventure.webs.com

Dedication

This book is dedicated to Patricia who is my Admiral, shipmate, best friend and wife. While in the Navy I learned that the Captain is responsible for the ship and its safe return, but the Admiral is the one that sends the Captain out to sea. Pat who is my Admiral has been by my side all my adult life and it is to her that I owe my thanks.

Pat has had several medical issues during our cruising days. First an old broken arm got infected and resulted in 3 surgeries to include a new plate and massive bone graph. The next adventure was on the way to La Paz Mexico, she broke her ankle and was laid up for 6 months on the boat.

But she is sticking with it and still on Sunnyside!

Table of Contents

The Basics

Chapter 1 – Selecting the Boat

After deciding to spend my retirement years cruising, I quickly learned that to assure the Admiral's continued support of that concept, there were features on a boat that she must have. I had not anticipated that boat features would be an important part of the plan. I was only interested in sailing to visit many places in the world. My wife, like many wives, had many requirements for the boat that focused on comfort on the trips and at anchor.

Regardless if it is the wife or husband driving this purchase, be sure and get the spouse's requirements factored in early, after all it is your home when aboard.

Types of Boats

There are several different types of Sailboats and Trawlers available to use for your cruising life home.

The simplest is the Sloop: A sloop has one mast and two sails. The forward sail is referred to as the headsail, Genoa or Jib. If the headsail does not go to the top of the mast it is called a fractional sloop. If it goes to the top it is a masthead it is just a sloop and those with a sail between the headsail and main are called a Cutter rig. The smaller stay sail can be very valuable in high wind and is frequently used instead of the head sail. It can also be very useful with the head sail for lighter winds to improve your speed through the water. A storm sail from that location also works much better than at the head of the boat, as it is more centered providing better balance for the boat.

Among all the sail boat styles there is also the option of having the cockpit in the approximate center of the boat or to the rear of the boat. It is normally assumed that the cockpit is aft and when it is a center cockpit typically has some abbreviation such as "cc" to differentiate it.

The sloop is a basic sailboat and maybe the most common style. Other styles have divided up the sail area into additional sails for traditionally more flexibility.

The Yawl is similar to a sloop, but has an additional mast installed aft of the rudder. Additional sails on a boat allow each sail to be physically smaller and more manageable. The second mast is called the mizzen mast. The attached picture shows the mizzen mast as about half the height of the main mast.

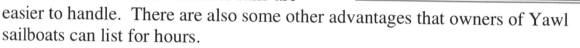

Most Yawl sail boats are larger boats that have a lot of sail area. Smaller sails are easier to handle. There are also some other advantages that owners of Yawl sailboats can list for hours.

If the same mast is moved forward of the rudder the boat is now called a Ketch. The sails are similar to the Yawl, but closer to the main.

They say that you can always tell a skipper that is sailing a ketch over one that sails a yawl as the skipper sailing the ketch with an aft cockpit is cross-eyed from staring directly into the mizzen mast. While that may not be 100% accurate, I am sure trying to look around the mizzen mast can get old.

The next type of boat we will discuss is the Schooner. The Schooner has two or more masts of the same height. The example shown has three masts. The after

mast would have functions similar to that of a ketch. Smaller Schooners only have two masts. Again, smaller sails are easier to rig and provide more flexibility for changing sailing conditions.

A boat of any size needs a defined amount of sail area to attain the maximum possible speed through the water. (Called Hull Speed) As we have discussed, this may be accomplished with two to many sails.

Another sailboat that is getting very popular is the Catamaran (Cat) style. Unlike the Mono Hull (single hull) boats, a Cat has two hulls. With two hulls Cats do not heal over (tilt) when under sail like a Mono hull does. As a result many folks have started cruising in a Cat.

Cats are also generally faster than equal sized Mono hulls when running (going with the wind) as the draft (how deep the hull goes into the water) on a Cat is typically less than a Mono Hull. They ride more on the surface of the water. A Cat can be about double the cost of a Mono Hull boat. A Cat resembles two boats tied together with a real nice pilot house in between.

There are many reasons that Cat owners can give you for why they are the best and an equal number of reasons why Mono Hull folks stick with them. I am myself allergic to Cats so I do not go there.

As sailors get older sometimes they gravitate toward the Trawler style powerboats. The Trawler is a diesel driven power boat that even though it has a small mast, there are no sails. The trawlers are built for comfort under power or at anchor.

Features and Fixtures

I have always liked the teak interior of a sailboat. The fact that many sailboats have small port lights and an overall dark appearance from the teak wood interior would never persuade me from a seaworthy vessel. My wife, on the other hand, could care less what the draft of the vessel is, but would like to make sure she can see outside when she is below decks. As she explains it, "I don't want to be in a tunnel" You should decide what you want in a boat before you start shopping. What you must have, what you would like to have and what you absolutely do not want.

"The Boat" shall be defined in this book as the boat you would like to buy.

The Basics List:

Must have, Nice to have, Could live with and Will not work list!

My income bracket required that I buy a used boat. In most cases, that is where the majority of cruising sailors are. Because the cost of buying a new boat is so high, used is frequently the best option. Buying a used boat has its advantages and disadvantages.

There are thousands of used boats available. That makes it important that you know what you want in a boat, before you start looking. You do not want to fall in love with a boat that will end up not working for your family and budget.

Buying a used boat is similar to buying a used house. The prior owners of a used house put in the trees and the landscaping, making it a nice place to live.

Likewise, when people buy new boats, they customize them to add features they want. For example, when we bought Sunnyside we got dishes, cups, knives, silverware, frying pans, kettles, lifejackets, cruising spinnaker, and even a significant number of spare parts for the engine and generator. That was in addition to the relatively new electronics they had installed on the boat and a new headsail. While the prior owner never got all his money back for all the great stuff he put on board, it was great to have it on board and saved me a lot of money.

To put this in perspective, a new 45 foot boat usually does not come standard with Radars, GPS, etc. A $500,000 boat can easily be $600,000-$700,000 before it is ready to go to sea.

Most dealers have a package you can purchase to get the boat ready for sea. When a boat leaves the yard the first time its value is similar to that of a new car. The value of that boat takes a major plunge, as the last line is cast off from where the boat was purchased.

The value of any electronics and other systems installed on the boat will rapidly approach zero dollar value. Clearly having the electronics onboard make a boat more desirable when purchasing a second hand boat. Selecting the right used boat can save you thousands of dollars if the used equipment works.

The Spouse's list

Before you start looking for your boat, it is important that you sit down with your spouse or crew to determine what he or she must have on the boat. A few questions you might ask that may help you create the proper list might include, but are not limited to the following:

1. How are we going to use the boat?
2. How many staterooms should we have?
3. How many heads do we need?
4. Do we want separate showers or a combined head and shower?
5. Should we have an oven in the galley?
6. What other appliances do we need?
7. Do we want a top opening or front opening refrigerator?
8. Do we want a deep freeze?
9. What should the inside look like?
10. Which cabins should be big rooms and which should be small?

After putting your spouse's list together, I would recommend that you initially put these items in the mandatory column.

Your List

Before making your list you should look at the technical side of the boat. Selecting the right size to fit your planned use is something you need to take seriously. I personally set 40 feet as the minimum size in which I was willing to sail in Open Ocean, but many sailors have done it in boats less than 30 feet. I would suggest the comfort factor of smaller boats was probably very low on those cruises, but the cost was equally low as a tradeoff.

When looking for a boat you should consider the basic design equations. They tell you a lot about the boat's capabilities vs. what you are planning. The equations are not the bottom line, but do serve as a general guideline to compare a boat's speed, comfort, etc. to your requirements.

Longer, wider and heavier sailboats often with deeper keels provide more stability under sail. Heavier sailboats are more comfortable, but may go slower. Shallow keels allow you to operate better and safer in shallow water, but may not sail into the wind as well. (Beat into the wind) A wing keel makes some improvements on the shallow keel's ability to beat into the wind and still have a small draft for shallow water.

When the sea is rough they all bounce around and may not be all that comfortable for some.

For your convenience the basic equations can be sent by me via email and are included in text format on the following pages. p-t_on_sunyside@live.com

After adding the specific boat information as in the examples, the spreadsheet completes the calculations and displays the appropriate numbers on the spreadsheet. You will not have to dig out and learn how to use a scientific calculator. See the file: "Buying the Boat.xls" Tab: "Calculations" Note: The data sheet has two sections. The left side is where you enter the data for the sheet and the answers are provided on the right. The worksheet is also protected so you do not accidentally change the calculations. See Appendix II for calculations.

The questions you need to address are much simpler and relative to your actual ability to safely transit the oceans and lakes you plan to visit.

1. How do you plan on using the boat? (It may be different than the spouse.)
2. How old a vessel do I want to take on? (This is important as the older it is, the more money you generally have to put in after the purchase to get it ready for sea.)
3. What electronics components must be included on the boat? (GPS, AIS, Radar, VHF radio, High Frequency SSB radio, EPRIB, new instruments, etc.)
4. What type of engine?
5. What do we want for entertainment electronics: TV (LCD or LED), Stereo, CD, DVD, etc.?
6. Are the sails less than 3 years old?
7. Length of boat?
8. Cockpit location (Center or aft)?
9. Type of boat you would like to sail (Sloop, Cutter, Yawl, Schooner, etc.)?
10. Boat construction (fiberglass, aluminum, steel, wood, wood trim, minimal wood, no wood)?

Some of the items you may want to look for and include in the negotiation when purchasing your boat are included in the lists below.

Starting at the bow - My top 38 external items would include:

1. Bow Thruster
2. One anchor with 100% chain
3. One anchor with chain and line
4. Anchor windless
5. Windless controls on deck or in cockpit
6. Roller feruled head sail(s)
7. Staysail rigging and sails
8. Fresh water hose or shower head at anchor chocks
9. Abandon ship life raft
10. Spinnaker and pole
11. Cleats amidships
12. 2 or 3 Reefs in the main sail
13. Boom Vang
14. All lines brought back to cockpit to enhance single handing
15. At least 2 mast mounted winches
16. Canvas dodger and Bimini or hard dodger and Bimini
17. Vinyl windows clear and usable
18. Cockpit mounted instruments
19. Cockpit mounted GPS
20. Hand Held GPS as backup
21. Cockpit VHF Radio
22. Spare VHF Radio
23. Auto Pilot large enough for boat
24. CARD (Collision Avoidance Radar Detector)
25. Waterproof speakers in Cockpit
26. Dingy
27. Motor for Dinghy
28. Motor lifting and stowing system
29. Davits to lift Dinghy onto the back of the boat
30. Swim platform
31. Cleat amidships aft to connect dinghy when towing
32. Backstay incorporates a SSB Antenna
33. Screw type (standard /folding)
34. Quality of dock lines
35. Solar Cells
36. Wind generator
37. Other energy sources
38. Other things?

Starting at the bow - My top 39 inside items would include

1. Size of V Birth
2. TV (LCD or tube) in V Birth
3. Fans in all Birth
4. Forward head with exhaust fan
5. Forward head includes separate shower
6. Heating system forward
7. Air conditioning forward
8. TV (LCD or LED) in Salon
9. Radio in Salon / Speakers
10. DVD or VCR in Salon (12 volts DC or 110 VAC)
11. Microwave (12 volts or 110 VAC) on gimbals
12. Stove/oven on gimbals for sea use
13. Engine heated and electrical hot water tank
14. Engine heat system
15. Diesel oil heating system (if the boat is used in northern waters)
16. Fresh water filter system installed
17. Water maker installed – GPH? (plan for at least 10-12 gallons per day per person when cruising.)
18. Sea water foot pump
19. Freshwater foot pump
20. Electrical system wiring neatly installed with modern electrical panels.
21. Digital meters on breaker panel
22. Battery quality measurement system
23. Separate house and starting battery banks
24. Diesel generator adequate to supply same power as shore power cables
25. Room for adequate batteries to provide 6 house batteries and 1 starting battery
26. Navigation station capable of laying out charts
27. Other Cabin requirements
28. Other head requirements
29. Engine hours meter
30. Pre-Fuel water and dirt filter system
31. Vacuum gauges on outlets of fuel filters
32. Generator hours meter
33. Drip-less seal on drive shaft
34. Aft heat system
35. Aft air conditioning system
36. Other TV or sound systems (LCD or tube type)
37. Master stateroom has own head with exhaust fan
38. Dishes and silverware supplied
39. Cooking items (pots, pans, utensils)

Consolidate your list before you start to look for the boat so you can keep your eye on the mission.

After you find the perfect boat, take the time to find some more just like it. You may be able to find the perfect boat at a competitive price if you spend the time.

Compromise

After forming your list you can start the fun part, looking at boats. After looking at a few boats it will result in modifications and compromises to your original requirements. After looking at 20-30 boats, you will be able to narrow the list down to one type of boat that provides the key features with minimum compromises.

While some your requirements will cost a lot of dollars to add and some may be just time you must spend, the cruising value must be considered before elimination from your list. If you have to add systems to the boat, it takes additional dollars beyond the price of the boat. Having something, even if it is a few years old, may be better than nothing to get started. Besides having lots of toys on the boat will give you things to fix when the weather is bad and as the boat ages.

Boats in my experience are all about compromise. We are looking for something that floats, is comfortable to live on, and takes heavy weather. The ideal safety at sea vessel might be a steel tube with no windows, but the ideal living conditions might be the house you are living in now with all the windows and doors. The boat that will be best for you is usually someplace in the middle.

People tend to look at the surface of something to evaluate the desirability of an item. I have included a list of the top 40 things inside and outside the boat you may want to consider when buying a cruising boat. Many items that the original owner purchased and used will help you get started if they are included in the deal. People selling their boats no longer need those items and you can obtain them during the negotiation at little or no cost.

Other things to consider:

1. Based on expected travel, fuel tank capacity
2. Based on expected travel, water tank capacity
3. Spare parts inventory (Take an inventory and check out the value of supplied components.)

Insurance

The larger the boat and the cruising area you plan to cruise in, the more boat insurance will cost. If you will be financing The Boat, the bank will require full coverage of at least the loan value on The Boat for the value financed.

The insurance goes up considerably for boats insured for more than the book value. The insurance industry does not like to cover anything for greater than the book listing, regardless of replacement cost.

Be sure that The Boat is a size you will still be able to afford and enjoy on a monthly basis after paying the insurance, slip fees, maintenance, and operating costs.

Check insurance rates on the web before you buy. It may seems like everyone sells boat insurance.

- http://boat-insurance-quotes-online.com/st-paul-fire-marine-insurance-company/
- http://www.boatus.com/insurance/
- http://www.americanboating.org/insurancehome.asp
- http://www.allboatinsurance.com/
- http://www.statefarm.com/insuranc/boat/boat.htm
- http://www.allstate.com/Products/Other/Boat/PageRender.asp?Page=main.htm
- http://www.boatowners.com/insurance.htm
- http://www.boatinsurancecanada.com/
- http://www.bluewaterins.com/

Our Insurance is with a great agent in San Diego, George Lindley. George takes great care of us anywhere and everywhere.
Phone: 612-222-2560   glindley@dksmarineinsurance.com

Moorage Considerations

Permanent and temporary moorage is based on how long the boat is or the slip ad if it is in a slip or on a mooring buoy. The majority of the time moorage is based on the higher of the two following calculations.

Length Overall times the rate, $/foot. In the Northwest we have reasonable rates of $2-5/foot, but I understand that some marinas in many other parts of the country are significantly higher. The length is not the same length as LOA of the boat. It typically includes your dingy hanging off the back, swim platforms, and bow sprits.

Some marinas charge for the larger of two calculations, slip size or boat size. So even if you have a 20 foot boat and you park it in a 50 foot slip, you may have to pay based on the 50 foot slip rate. If you hang over, it could cost you even more.

Always try to negotiate what you pay, especially if there are a lot of slips open at the marina of choice. Unfortunately, it is more common to have a long waiting list instead of open slips which reduces your negotiation ability. That typically means, "Take it or leave it!" as far as the price, but it never hurts to ask.

Operation and Maintenance

When buying a boat the cost of new equipment, repair parts and operating costs are directly proportional to the length of the boat. For example, fuel will cost the same per gallon for all boats, assuming the same type of engine. (Diesel or gas) However, the larger the boat is the more fuel it will take to push it around. Another example is the larger the boat the larger the pieces that go on the boat. One of my first experiences was knocking off the bow light on my boat. I looked in my favorite catalogue and found what I believed to be the replacement for only $40. Upon arriving at the boat store with my broken one in hand, I found that the price was about $80. My light was significantly larger than the $40 fixture I thought I had found in the catalogue which was actually for boats less than 40 feet.

Boaters claim there is a new currency called the boat dollar. A boat dollar is about $1,000 for boats over 40 feet. So when you go to West Marine, if you think it is worth a buck, it will be a grand before you have all the parts.

Much of the additional cost for parts and materials stems from the design requirements for boat parts. We like to use rust resistant stainless steal for metal, leak proof products, waterproof, and spark resistant. Even the wire we use is special as it should be tinned strands of copper wire. The tinning will resist corrosion of the copper strands. All that costs money to build and our small group of boaters has to pay the higher cost.

As stated before an item for a 30 foot boat might cost $50, that same item must be bigger on a 40 foot boat. As a result it could cost $100 for the 40 foot boat.

As with the insurance and moorage, be sure that The Boat is a size you will still be able to afford and enjoy on a monthly basis after operating and maintenance costs.

The Negotiation for The Boat

This section is discussed but should be skipped if you have unlimited funds and do not care what you pay for the boat.

When negotiating for the boat or anything else for that matter, I always say the one with the most data wins. Even before you have the boat surveyed, you will have a lot of information about the boat. Basic strategy I would recommend is, don't get caught up in having to have the one boat that you are looking at right now. There are a lot of boats out there, so don't focus on any one unless the deal is right. For guys and gals it is like your dream girl or guy. If they say no interest, there are a lot of other great people out there who may even be better and more compatible. So be willing to stand firm on your price and any extras you would like them to throw in to the deal. I always say "It never hurts to ask".

Negotiation Rule One

Do not be afraid to walk away from any deal. There are thousands of boats for sale and many like the one you are looking at, and maybe even better.

Do your homework. If you were buying a home you would get estimates of the type of home you are looking at. So get lots of prices on comparable boats all over the US and Canada before you start making offers. Look in magazines, on the web, etc., to find pricing on similar boats with similar features. Get data on other boats made a few years on either side of the year of The Boat. Make a list of the features for each boat. The disk provided with the book shows an example of how to compare features and years. See file: "Buying the Boat.xls" Tab: "Features&Price"

A few web sites you may want to check out to find market prices that I used include:

- http://www.yachtworld.com/
- http://www.powerandsailboatsforsale.com/
- http://www.48north.com/
- http://www.boattrader.com/

Here is also an interesting idea. A sail boats for sale forum: http://boatdiesel.com/Forums/main.cfm?cfapp=53&Forum_ID=202

One tactic I have used for years to buy things like cars and my present boat has been to show only the boats that are a few years older and newer. Then I calculate the average for each year. Then I scale the older and newer boats to a number for the year of The Boat I am looking at to identify the boat's market value.

The boats selected should have comparable features, but the ones in your spreadsheet (used to show the dealer) would be the lowest priced boats you can find with similar features. This will provide you with the bottom number for your negotiation. Start with evidence that you know what the boat is really worth. During the negotiations, *The Boat* should show the lowest market value possible.

When I bought my car that way, the dealer said he would sell the car to me at that price, but I had to give him a copy of the spreadsheet to close the deal.

Negotiation Rule two

Get the numbers that the banks will use for the make, model and year of *The Boat*. Ask the bank or a dealer for the book price. If the asking price for the boat you are looking at is higher than the book value, as is always the case, be sure and have that number displayed and discussed during the negotiations.

The Boat's book value is a creditable third party source and says the boat is worth less than the asking price. While you may never come close to this typically really low value for *The Boat*, it can help you drag down the seller's idea of what *The Boat* is worth.

Negotiation Rule Three

I am sure you have heard the happiest days in boating are when you buy the boat and when you sell the boat. Keeping that in mind, the person that wants to sell the boat has reasons. Try to find out what is driving the need to sell.

A few things to find out from the broker before making an offer:
- How long it has been since he or she sailed the boat?
- When are the slip fees due again?
- Any other offers been made, if so why did they fall through?
- What did the previous owner use the boat for?
- How long did he or she own it?
- How many owners did the boat have?
- Who did the service on the boat?
- Who did the upgrades?

The above information can be extremely useful in the negotiation process. For example if the present owner has a $1000 bill coming due next month to store a boat he no longer wants, his price will be more flexible. If the owner has not used the boat in a year, bid low and negotiate. If the boat is ten years old and has had three or four owners, bid real low, negotiate or maybe select another boat. Again, look for the reasons the owner wants to sell. Figure out how you're buying the boat "now" is to the owner's advantage and you will get the best buy.

The Negotiation

I had a budget in mind when I started the process to buy Sunnyside. The boat I wanted was listed at $25,000 more than I wanted to pay for a boat. I showed my calculations to the broker and he told the seller. This really set the stage for the negotiation.

The seller had to pay summer storage in New England soon and wanted to sell now. He got a bit upset with the offer, but wanted to sell badly so become very flexible. The $2000 bill coming due for summer storage pushed him into a

$25,000 discount. Granted I could have gotten a $10,000 discount for just making an offer of $120,000, but $105,000 is what I wanted to pay and did. An 8% discount would have been good, but a 20% discount was even better as it turned out.

Show your calculation sheet to the broker. Let the broker discuss the sheet and the offer with the present owner. It may end up as a win/win for everyone. Don't forget that the broker could trim his commission if he is sure you have the dough to close.

Based on my sheet I was able to purchase the boat with little negotiation. The owner would have liked to get the $25,000 more for the boat, but it had been on the hard for at least six months, he had bought a restaurant, had little time to sail, and had a rental fee for the space he was taking up on the hard coming due the following month. These are all things to find out and take into consideration in a negotiation.

It was worth 20% off list to know all the data. Four years later, boats similar to mine are still listed in the market for more than I paid. It was a win/win for both of us. The price I had in mind before doing all the calculations was the upper limit I could afford, $105,000. I needed to be at the $105,000 in order to have the cash to add the other items I needed to get the boat home. Dinghy, dinghy motor, life raft, GPS, supplies, etc.

When I used this technique on the car I bought I saved almost 30% on that deal. So I did not come out as good on my boat. However, to close that deal, I had to give the dealer a copy of the spreadsheet so he could save money on things he wanted to buy.

Chapter 2 – The Boat

Overview

When I was on submarines, there was an extreme emphasis on knowing everything possible about the submarine we were on to make sure everyone on board remained as safe as possible. Qualifications program meant you were able to draw and operate every system on the boat so that in an emergency we could take the appropriate action to stay alive. At sea on a sail boat means that you have to be prepared and know your boat.

If you plan to go cruising as a couple, you both need to know the boat and get "Qualified" on your vessel. To go to sea and not know your boat in the dark could result in not coming back. If something bad happens, this is not the time to start learning your systems, even on a little sailboat. So make it a top priority to know your boat and what makes it work. Know the normal sounds your boat makes, damage control techniques and survival techniques before you head for the big water. Know where every valve, wire run, switches, fire extinguisher, etc. is located.

One of the first things to do when you purchase your boat is to find out where all the valves that go through the hull are located. These holes are potentials for leaks big enough to sink your boat. (Later we will discuss what to do if one of those holes is leaking water into your boat.)

The second priority should be to trace each and every system on your boat. The hand over hand method works well, even though it can be very time consuming. As you trace each system, make a simple drawing of the system so you can refer to it once in a while to jog your memory. I did not have an expensive drawing system, so I used Power Point presentation software to create drawings for my boat. While they are not the greatest drawings, they are accurate and provide an excellent format to explain to new crew members how my boat works. Having the vessel's drawings on your computer will allow you to easily make changes after upgrades and/or modifications to the boat's systems. Drawings can also be very good to use as a training aid when you get new crew on board for a trip. We will discuss the basics of major systems in more detail in later chapters.

Every sound should mean something to you. You might ask "How do you learn that?" Well the answer is simple; spend time on your boat, even while at the dock. When you hear a noise you do not recognize, find out what it is and what caused it. I have learned the sounds of filters clogging, check valve stuck open in the bilge pump, and the latest is the high charge mode on my new Balmar alternator. Most of the strange sounds took some time to find, but now I am able to pick them out and hopefully avoid a potential problem.

Eventually you will learn to treat every grouping of equipment or functions as a system. The systems you might find on a typical sail boat that is ready for cruising would include:

➢ Standing rigging	➢ Cooling water system for Engine and Generator
➢ Running rigging	➢ Refrigeration
➢ Sails	➢ Fuel cleaning
➢ Engine	➢ Toilets (Head)
➢ Battery system	➢ Heat and air conditioning
➢ Charging System	➢ GPS
➢ AC System - Generator	➢ AIS
➢ AC System - Inverter System	➢ Radar
➢ Shore Power	➢ Instruments
➢ Fresh Water System	

Standing rigging

Standing rigging are all the pieces of the sailboat above the deck that keep the mast erect. This is an area that has caused a few friends some real grief when their mast broke and fell into the water.

Standing rigging is similar to the guy wires on a TV antenna. Their job is to keep the mast at approximately 90° to the top of the boat. In the case of a sail boat, there are a lot of forces that can all of a sudden change to the opposite direction. For example if the wind is pulling your sail and as a result it is bending your mast slightly. Then the wind changes to the other side and the mast suddenly is bent in the opposite direction. The stays and shrouds must be tight enough to support the changes in stress to minimize movement of the mast.

The Lines running fore and aft are called stays and are responsible for keeping the mast from moving too far in that plane. These lines normally extend to the top of the mast. The lines on the port and starboard side of the mast are called shrouds and are responsible for the same function as the fore and back stays, but side to side.

If you have ever taken physics and were exposed to the term momentum. Momentum of the mass and speed of movement of the mast as the mast shifts from one side to the other is what causes all the damage. A mast can have lots of momentum during an accidental jibe. Restricting the amount of movement by properly tensioned standing rigging may just save your mast. (An accidental jibe causes the boom for the main sail to swing from one side to the other very fast and then stop- a lot of potentially destructive energy)

Many sailors tend to tune their standing rigging for their boat way too loose. That means the mast can move a lot for wind shifts which increases the potential for mast destruction.

Get a tension gauge for your new boat or have someone who has tuned a lot of masts to help you. Don't let a little shift in the wind create a real bad day for you and your bank account. There are plenty of things to spend money on your boat, and there is no sense in wasting it on things that should be working fine.

Running Rigging

As you might have expected, running rigging are all the lines that allow you to sail the boat. This includes Halyards, Sheets, Reefing lines, Vang, Traveler, Outhaul, Cunningham, and preventer.

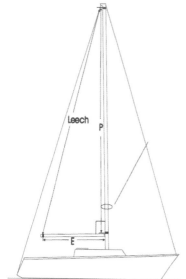

It is assumed that if you own a sail boat, you know how to use your running rigging. If not, enroll in a sailing school or at least find a friend who knows how to sail and invite him or her out with you. Beware of people who really have only been out once with someone else who knows how to sail. Find a friend with a boat.

The condition of the running rigging is almost as critical as standing rigging. Frayed lines can break and with out running rigging it can be very difficult to sail anywhere. The worst nightmare is breaking a line that is inside your mast. It is a lot easier to replace a frayed line than to fish in and pull a new line.

Frequent inspection of your rigging is advised. It may just eliminate a lot of potential cost, pain and misery.

Sails

Your sails will be the main engine of your sailboat. I guess that is why they call it sailing. While sails do not require fuel like other engines they do require a stable platform, must be in good condition and, hey, how about some wind!

Just like the rigging on a boat, using the sails will result in fraying of the material and eventually tears. The old saying that comes to mind is you can pay me now or a whole lot more later. The key to keeping your main engine running is to inspect the sails frequently for wear. When wear is found, fix it now.

Early in our sailing career, my wife and I bought a Sailrite sewing machine. The primary purpose was to repair sails if and/or when they became damaged. As it turned out we have used that machine for many things, but have only made minor repairs to the main sail and sail bag. These machines are tough and will sew through a very thick piece of material. We have used the machine to repair our canvas, make cushions, and even sew up some pants I bought that were too long. The machines may also be used for plain material, if you purchase the smaller needles.

Engine

While we are supposed to be sailors, we end up using that iron sail a lot more than most of would like to think. You will find yourself on the engine when there is no wind and you do not have the time to allow for waiting for the wind, when in strong currents in rivers and going up river, etc.

If you are planning to use your boat for Cruising, it will be equipped with a diesel engine (hopefully) large enough that it will allow you to achieve close to your hull speed for your boat. It is important that you learn to maintain your engine as service calls in the ocean are expensive if even possible. For me this was a new experience. Since my background has been electronics and electricity, the thought of working on a diesel engine was a bit scary.

As it turns out diesel engines are simple. They need air, water and fuel to run and they just keep on running like the Eveready bunny. Making sure water, air and clean fuel are available, will keep your engine running. Later we will discuss the types of things you should consider doing to assure the engine is there for you when you need it.

Battery system

The battery system is a critical system on a sailboat. While you are sailing, the batteries will be used and eventually discharged requiring that energy be put back in via some external source. The battery system will be discussed in great detail in a later chapter.

Charging System

Charging is a significant factor in successful cruising if you want electricity. The 12 volts DC (the battery) electricity is really a necessity for cruising as all the instruments, lights and the GPS run off the 12VDC system. To minimize the cost of charging your batteries you need to charge them as efficiently as possible. If you need to run the engine a lot, you might as well have a power boat.

With a significant number of amp-hours in most cruising house battery systems, charging is a critical subject. The original equipment on most boats may include 200-300 amp-hours of house battery. That is not very much when you are trying to stay off the engine. The factory installed alternator was typically sized for the 200-300 amp-hour batteries. As a result the installed alternator will never keep up with charging a larger 500 to 800 amp-hours house battery in a reasonable time period, if ever. Charging systems details and strategies will be discussed in a later chapter.

AC System

Generator

The Alternating Current system is the 110-125V system on your boat that resembles the outlets in your house. In fact when you are tied to a dock and plugged into shore power, there is little difference and the power may come from the same power company that supplies your house.

Unfortunately, long extension cords to the dock would make it a bit tough to sail across an ocean or even rivers. The 120 volts AC may be supplied on board by an onboard generator or another device called an inverter. The inverter converts the 12 volts DC to 120 volts AC and will be discussed in the next section.

Basically: An AC generator is similar to what the utilities use to generate the electricity that is provided at your shore power connection. On the boat a generator is normally a rotating machine driven by an engine similar to the one that pushes the boat. The basic concept is that a rotating shaft with coils of wire on the shaft (the rotor windings) develops a rotating magnetic field inside the generator. The field is as a result of current passing through the brushes to the rotor windings. The developed field passes by another set of coils and induces a voltage signal into them. The stationary coils are called the stator windings. The voltage out of the stator is proportional to both the energy applied from the engine and the field in the rotor. The voltage and current applied to the rotor create a magnetic field and the amount of field is determined by a regulator. (More than you ever needed to know about generators!)

Not all boats have generators, but most cruising boats do. The generator is responsible for supplying 120 Volts AC to run microwaves, coffee pots, air conditioners, heaters, etc. Our boat, Sunnyside, has an 8 KW generator. The 8KW generator will supply enough energy to replace the 60 amps that are available on our two shore power connection.

What size? If you only have one 30 amp shore power cord you may replace all of that energy with a generator of 3,600 watts (4KW generator), two 30 amp connections would then require at least 7,200 watts (8KW). Your power needs and the space on your boat will set the requirements and ultimately capabilities for 120 volts AC on your boat. Keep in mind that if you are planning to install a generator that a little reserve makes sense, but putting an 8KW generator on a boat that has one 30 amp shore power connection will just burn extra fuel and take up extra valuable space on board. Having too small a generator will result in tripping breakers and possible damage to the generator.

The generator will require maintenance similar to the maintenance required by the engine. One key difference I learned the hard way is you need to run the generator once in a while. If you do not, the brushes can get corroded and the generator engine will not continue to run. I put in a lot of hours determining why the engine would start and then stop when I released the start button. While it was a painful experience at the time, it was a good training session for me as I learned a lot about engines and generators throughout the exercise. The tough part was that the generator was behind the hot water heater. The water heater had to be removed to gain access to the generator and the brushes.

To eliminate the problem of corroding brushes, I run the generator at least once a month, under a load such as the hot water heater, to clean off the brushes. I have not had the problem repeat over the past 10 years.

Inverter System

The inverter is an electronic system that uses 12 volt battery energy to develop a sine wave output similar to that from a generator. Some units provide a very good clean sine wave and some do a very poor job. So be sure you spend your money wisely to meet your needs.

The 12 volts DC voltage is stepped up to 120 volts AC and made available for household appliances like microwaves, coffee pots, TVs, margarita blenders, etc..

There are no moving elements in an inverter. The inverter is an electronic device. The key thing to remember on an inverter is the wattage ratting. A 1000 watt inverter may run a coffee pot, but not your microwave. Typically only one large appliance may be run from your inverter at a time.

The basics of how an inverter works: Electronic switches turn the battery 12 volts DC on and off at a 60 cycles per second rate (60 Hz), the current is run through a device called a transformer to create a voltage approximately 10 times that of the 12 volt battery.

Typical inverters can be purchased as small units to drive a TV (100's of watts), 1000 watts, 1500 watts, 2000 watts, 2500 watts, etc. Please review the following table to better understand the impact of inverters on your battery.

Inverter Sizing Table

Inverter size	~ Available Amps	Can be used for	~ Battery draw
100 Watts	1.2 Amps	Small appliance	12 Amps
1000 Watts	8 Amps	Coffee Pot or Microwave	80 Amps
1500 Watts	12.5 Amps	Larger Coffee pot or Microwave	125 Amps
2000 Watts	16 Amps	Coffee Pot and Microwave at the same time	160 Amps
2500 Watts	20.8 Amps	Most appliances	208 Amps

(Based on an output of 120 Volts AC)

Fresh Water System

Fresh water is something that is absolutely required on a boat. Most boats have large fresh water tanks, in fact often larger than the fuel tank. People generally use an average of about 10 gallons of water per person per day. This includes washing dishes, cooking, showers, and consumption.

To make sure you do not get sick from the water on aboard, adding about a 1/4 cup of plain Clorox bleach per 100 gallons of water will make sure the critters will not make you sick. Some folks also use iodine, which has no taste, but requires a lot more at a higher cost. To eliminate the chlorine from the drinking water, use a filter on the main supply and then a charcoal filter attached to the faucet. There "ain't" nothing getting through there but H2O.

Do you need a water maker? This depends on how you plan to travel. For lake, river and coastal cruising in the US, the water tanks will probably be sufficient to maintain an adequate supply of water on your boat. If you do not plan on pulling into a marina though or traveling to other countries, you may want to install a water maker. If your plans include transiting across the ocean, then plan for a water maker that will make adequate water for the crew while not draining your batteries.

Another consideration for a water maker is if you will be going into ports, anchoring away from shore (on the hook) and having to carry multiple 6 gallon containers from shore in the dingy to fill your 200 gallon tank. I understand if you are cruising with two strong teenage children, dingy water service is still the best approach. For two old folks, you may want a watermaker.

Cooling water system for Engine and Generator

The cooling water system on my boat was a lot more complex than I ever dreamed of. It is more than just a once through passage of sea water doing a once through cooling of a freshwater heat transfer mechanism (a water cooled heat exchanger (radiator) inside the engine).

The components of a more complex cooling system includes: hull valve, strainer, pump, cooling coils, mixing valve, muffler system, and finally back over the side with the exhaust. The mixing valve mixes the hot exhaust with the now warm cooling water and cools the exhaust being sent to the muffler system. The muffler system has hoses that are elevated above the waterline and finally the exhaust goes overboard. The big failure items here are clogged strainer, the worn out rubber impellers (pump wheel) and holes in the mixing valve as a result of heat changes, corrosion etc.

The freshwater parts of the cooling system are very similar to those in your car's cooling system; heat exchanger, closed loop, and expansion tank. The heat exchanger can develop leaks over time as a result of the corrosive effect on the cooling tubes from the combination of heat, cold, and salt water interacting. Just like in your car, don't forget to keep the expansion tank at the full level mark.

Refrigeration

It seems like every now and then someone is stranded someplace because the refrigeration unit went out on the boat. There are several types of refrigeration systems that include AC, DC, and engine driven units.

The refrigeration cycle basics are simple. You pressurize a Freon type gas (R11, R12 etc.) into a small tube and it becomes a liquid in the process. The liquid is routed to the piece in the refrigerator or deep freeze that you want to make cold. A spray nozzle is located in the piece of equipment that freezes and then the liquid is sprayed out, losing its pressure. When Freon goes to atmospheric pressure it boils sucking up all the heat at that location. The vapor is fed back to a cooling element and placed back in the reservoir to be re-used.

The big difference of refrigeration systems on boats is how you cool and how you create the pressure.

➤ Pressure can be created by your engine or a pump, but some how you need to add energy to the gas to get it to go back to a high pressure liquid.
➤ Cooling can be done with air or seawater.

Fuel cleaning

There are always built in filters on diesel engines. Again diesels need air, cooling water and clean fuel to run properly. All the rest is magic. Actually there is a bit more to it and we will discuss later.

Diesel fuel tanks draw moisture and somehow get little bugs in there that grow. So even if you use a fuel filter when filling your tank(s) (real good idea in a lot of places), you need to filter the fuel and remove water before sending the fuel to the engine. It is also important that you use a product in the fuel to kill the bugs such as "BioGuard" by ValvTech.

Going through rough water will kick up all the bad stuff in the bottom of the tank, clog the filter and kill the engine. Losing your engine in rough water is not a fun thing to happen. Been there, done that. Having a spare filter already installed can be a real life saver. The miserable alternative is to change out filters in the middle of a rough ocean. Changing a fuel filter in a cramped space in rough seas can be real challenging, plus presents a high potential for sea sickness.

I highly recommend that all ocean going boats install a second filter that allows you to switch filters.

There are a lot of expensive products on the market that will provide a complete cleaning station. As an alternative you can buy two Racor water separating filters, some hose valves, and T connections. You must have that second filter, for when the one on line clogs, the engine will not run. Another frequent mistake is buying a filter that just exceeds your requirements. When the dirt kicks up it can clog the filter quickly. I would recommend the use of the largest Racor filters possible. Using a larger filter will increase the filter surface area to reduce the possibility of clogging during rough seas.

I put three valves at the fuel tank access (you have to reach them while the engine is running). One valve for each filter input and one valve as a bypass of the two filters, for use in an emergency. I figured the bypass line still has the original equipment filter to protect the engine for a short time.

While it is not really a cleaning topic, it is a very good idea to have a fuel pump at the output of the fuel filters. It not only helps you prime the engine, but if a filter gets clogged, it can buy you time to suck fuel through a clogged filter for a few minutes.

Regardless of what you use for a filter, be sure you have a vacuum gauge on the output so you can determine the status of the fuel filter on line. If the filter is clogged, the engine sucking on it trying to get fuel will create a vacuum in the line between the filter and the engine.

Toilets / The Head

This can be a dirty subject. There are a lot of different types of heads (toilet by the home name), but the basics are the same. You need to provide flushing water, typically a hull valve, and the waste goes someplace else. Some folks like to use their fresh water as the smell is better, but that will increase the required fresh water you make or haul from shore. Seawater can have marine life, bacteria, and other waste in it that can create smells.

Some marine toilets have a mechanism in them to chop up the waste and move it to a tank. This can be an electric motor, or like on our boat, we get our exercise each day by using the hand pump. There are also vacuum operated heads like on airplanes, but I figure the exercise is good for sailors.

The head dumps into a holding tank and the tank may be pumped out or discharged overboard if off shore at least 12 miles. Some boats also have a valve that allows you to go directly overboard, but that valve is supposed to be locked or at least strapped shut when within the 12 mile limit.

Chemicals to keep the head holding tank from smelling can be very expensive. We have found the best value for the chemicals is using RV toilet chemicals. The RV industry does a great job and because of the number of RVs on the road, the chemicals are reasonably priced.

Heat and air conditioning

If you have an air-conditioner on board or a heat pump, they work similarly to the refrigeration. The heat pump shifts to which energy it wants to use in the system when changing from heat to cool. Remember the cycle, it cools one piece by absorbing the heat into the Freon when it vaporizes and then when the Freon is cooled, it removes the heat to the air or water. A heat pump in effect selects which part of the cycle it wants to use, and where it wants to dump the heat. In a cooling cycle it extracts the heat out of the unit and dumps it into the water. For the heat cycle, it tries to cool the water, extracts the heat out of the water, and then transfers it into the boat.

Other heat sources include diesel heaters, engine hot water heaters, propane heaters and some folks even use wood burning or pellet heaters.

GPS

Most people today are familiar with GPS. We have it in cars, hand units for hiking and many other applications. Thank you US Navy for this fantastic tool. I was actually associated with some of the early satellite navigation systems while I was in the Navy, but today's GPS and differential GPS provide accuracies we never thought possible.

When you tie the GPS into a chart plotter and add electronic charts, it is like a video game except it is you on the screen. As a result we do not even pay much attention to Latitude, Longitude, heading and speed as the chart shows us where we are all the time.

Adding AIS to the chart plotter, adds the large ships on the GPS display and some smaller vessels. AIS collects and displays a significant amount of information to help with collision avoidance. More information on AIS is provided later.

The thing to think about is what do I do if the GPS dies? Keeping a log of Lat/Lon/Compass heading/Course over ground and Speed over ground from the GPS are real nice to have when the GPS dies. It is always good to plot onto hard copy. Don't let the fantastic GPS technology turn you into a casualty when it crashes or the sea is too rough to use, and it will happen if you go to sea.

Radar

While many boats seem to do just fine without radar, my advice is, "Don't Leave Home Without It". Going into the ocean without radar can be a lot like walking down a county road with a blind fold on.

When the night is pitch black and the only thing you can see is your own lights, when the fog is so thick you cannot see your own lights, and even when there are just a lot of vessels around it is very comforting to have radar on board.

The next important thing is to know how to use it. It just takes practice to learn to operate the radar effectively. Practice at the dock: pick out objects such as points of land or buoys that you can see. Then using the radar, determine the range and bearing to each object. Also try tracking boats going by your marina and figure out how far from you they will be when they get to the closest to you, the Closest Point of Approach (CPA).

Learn the controls and different functions for your radar, and then take it to sea because "if it is going to happen, it will happen out there."[1]

There is more on Radar later, but in case you could use some help, I have posted a Radar training presentation I did in Ensenada Mexico in 2009 at:

http://sunnyside-adventure.webs.com/trainingforsailors.htm

There is also some training on Communications and DC power for those that want to learn even more. Should you want some help with the slides, contact me at p-t_on_sunyside@live.com and we can meet on Skypes for some training. If you are un-aware of Skypes, check that out also. It is a great cruising tool. http://www.skype.com

Radar can also be used to obtain position fixes. Pick a point off a chart; locate it on the radar and note time, distance, and bearing. Plot it and that is where you are. You can also use two points and take two ranges or two bearings and where they cross is where you are. It is worth playing with in the event that your GPS is no longer functioning and you are within radar range of land.

---

1. Favorite quote from the famous sailing movie "Captain Ron"

Instruments

Instruments are the devices we use to measure our surroundings and display information in the cockpit. Typical devices measure and display wind, speed through water, depth, heading, temperature, rudder angle, etc.

Modern systems also combined the measurements with a communications network so that along with GPS and radar information, they can be displayed in several locations and be available for use by other devices such as an auto pilot so that it knows where to steer.

One thing to consider with the speed through water instrument is the need to pull the instrument out of the hull from the inside to clean off the collected crud. On the original unit on Sunnyside, we ended up with a couple of gallons of water inside the boat each time the paddle wheel was removed and the plug put in. I always had to fight the one foot fountain back with the dummy plug. After cleaning the transducer (paddle wheel that senses the movement through water), I had my second shot at stopping the fountain and a couple of more gallons of water in the boat. My sailing buddy use to say, "Wow that was impressive" every time I went through the exercise.

My new Raymarine unit has a rubber flapper that is pushed up into the hole when the transducer is pulled out. Since the stream is only a few inches high now, I only get about a quart of water inside for each change. It is a good deal that Raymarine and others have incorporated the simple rubber flapper!

Enhancing the Skills

Boat Systems
Chapter 3 – Sails

When I first started sailing, no one really talked about sail dimensions. After I bought Sunnyside, sail/mast dimensions seemed to pop up all the time. It is easy with the internet to determine what everyone was talking about.

Before looking at the sail areas and calculations, be sure and review chapter one again to make sure you know which sail is which.

The following definitions and calculations are provided as a ready reference so you do not have to go look them up.

Sail and Mast Dimensions:

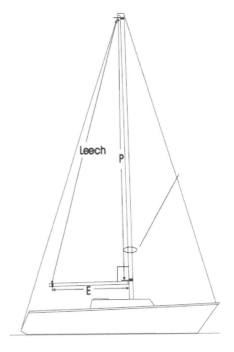

I = Height of head stay termination above the sheer line. In other words "I" is measured along the front of mast from the Genoa halyard to the main deck. The main deck is where the deck would be if there were no deckhouse.

J = Distance between the head stay termination at the deck and the front of the mast at the sheer line. Or "J" may be defined as the base of the fore triangle measured along the deck from the head stay pin to the front of the mast.

P = Distance between black bands on the mast, or the maximum luff length of the main sail or in other words the luff is the length of the mainsail, measured along the aft face of the mast from the top of the boom to the highest point that the mainsail can be hoisted or to the black band. (The front side)

E = Distance between black bands on the boom, or the maximum foot length of the main sail. E can also be defined as the foot length of the mainsail, measured along the boom from the aft face of the mast to the outermost point on the boom to which the main can be pulled or to the black band.

PY & EY are similar to P & E, but indicate mizzen dimensions

"JSP" is the length of the spinnaker pole or the distance from the forward end of the bowsprit (fully extended) to the front face of the mast.

"ISP" is measured from the highest spinnaker halyard to the deck.

"PY" and "EY" are, respectively the luff length and foot length of the mizzen of a yawl or ketch measured in the same way as for the mainsail.

"IY" is the measurement from the staysail halyard to the deck.

"JY" is the measurement from the staysail stay to the front face of the mast.

"LP" is the shortest distance between the clew and the luff of the Genoa.

Sail Area Calculations

The following equations are approximations of sail areas.

- ◈ Mainsail Area $= P \times E / 2$
- ◈ Headsail Area $= (\text{Luff} \times \text{LP}) / 2$
  (LP is the shortest distance between the clew and the luff)
- ◈ Approx. 150% Genoa Area $= (1.5 \times J \times I) / 2$
- ◈ Approx. 135% Genoa Area $= (1.35 \times J \times I) / 2$
- ◈ 100% Fore triangle $= (I \times J) / 2$
- ◈ Approx. Spinnaker Area $= 1.8 \times J \times I$

Sail Type

There are a lot of choices when you start replacing your sails. Some sails are very high tech with many small pieces of material going in many directions. While some of the new fabrics will probably make you go faster, cruising sails are all about strength and longevity. I prefer sails with double stitched Dacron. Sunnyside came with a Doyle main sail that was 13 years old and after 16 years it was still in reasonably good shape. It has remained dependable and now that I am purchasing a new sail from Doyle, I plan to put the old one in storage just in case I get into trouble in the South Pacific or some other place far, far away.

There are many complete books on sails, so get one that includes material types and sail maintenance. If you think you need to buy a new sail, read up on sails first. You will find there is a lot to sails. Also, check out reviews in sailing magazines like Practical Sailor (www.practicalsailor.com). Be sure and talk to others who have bought sails recently and check out the internet before establishing a contract with any vendor. The key to success is research before you buy. Research will result in a better buying and sailing experience.

There are many local sail makers that may be as good as or maybe even better than Doyle where I bought my sail. With my center cockpit limiting my access to the boom area, I favored the Doyle stack pack as well as the quality I have seen as displayed by my prior sail's 15 years of good service.

Chapter 4 – Diesel Engine

The Engine

A diesel engine is a great thing to have on a boat. Unlike the gasoline engines on many power boats, the explosive fumes are not present for diesel engines. A diesel engine also has a simple operating cycle, high efficiency, and long life.

Maintenance on a diesel engine is also minimal. Key maintenance <u>is keeping</u> the fuel clean and making sure that air is available. So make sure the air and fuel filters are clean and the engine will run. It is also very important to change the oil as recommended. I change mine every 3-4 months even with minimal use. The filter should be changed at the same time. I would expect that the newer engines require a different level of maintenance than the engines prior to 1990. With the implementation of diesel engines in cars and trucks, consumers demanded less smoke and easier operation. My 1987 Yanmar smokes a lot, but that is just the way it is. As long as it maintains a blue smoke, I am good to go. (Smoke color is discussed later.)

How a Diesel engine cycles.

1. Piston withdraws from all the way up.
2. The valve opens and the air comes in.
3. The valve then shuts.
4. Piston starts moving back up.
5. The piston compresses the air held in the cylinder.
6. Compression of the air in the cylinder causes the air to heat.
7. The fuel injector shoots fuel into the cylinder filled with hot air.
8. The hot air and fuel combine and explode.
9. The energy of the explosion drives the piston back down.
10. The cycle starts all over again.

The key to remember and think about if you have engine troubles is that a diesel engine needs Fuel, Air, compression and timing. Since compression and timing do not typically change and the air usually gets to the engine, the problem is most likely lack of Fuel. Clogged filters usually stop the flow of fuel and cause the engine to stop.

Fuel

➤ Need to keep it clean and reduce water as much as possible.
➤ Use BioGuard to kill bugs. Bugs lie between water and diesel fuel. Better to use too much BioGuard than not enough.
➤ Don't use any other additives for diesel engines.

Filters

➤ Use 2-micron Racor filter and you will not have to ever change the engine filter. Use a large filter unit to make sure the surface area will allow for crud being sucked up during heavy seas. I like the Racor R20S as it has lots of surface area.
➤ Install a Vacuum gauge on the outlet of the filter so you can see when your filter is getting clogged. When the filter is getting full, the vacuum will increase to about 10" of mercury.
➤ If your filter clogs in rough sea, put the second one in parallel with the first to allow maximum surface area for crud from the tank. With luck you will not fill both of them.

A Diesel Engine that Smokes

Smoke can come from inadequate air supply. Open the doors on the engine compartment and see if it goes away. Smoke can be a result of buildup at the exhaust's output and will go away after the engine is run for a while.

For Yanmar's built during the years 1970-80s they just have smoke. Most engines during that period had smoke. When Diesel engines started being used in cars, folks did not like the smoke. As a result newer designed engines significantly reduced the amount of smoke.

When we talk about smoke we are talking about the blue smoke. Blue smoke is common for engines developed before the 1990s. You should be concerned when ever you have black smoke for any year engine. Black smoke may be as a result of engine problems and should be checked out by an expert.

Props and Screws

The propeller, or screw as properly called, is the thing that pushes your boat along. The screw must be sized properly for your boat's engine. The size is a combination of two things: the diameter of the screw and the pitch of the screw. For a given diameter the screw will take more loading as the pitch is increased similarly to the way an airplane prop works.

When an airplane is "feathering its prop," it is not pulling the airplane forward or pushing it aft. As the pitch is increased it pulls the airplane forward or aft.

The same is true for a boat screw. However, too much pitch will load the engine too heavily and not increase your speed. Too little will result in too little speed!

The screw is a critical piece for boat horsepower to transfer to the water. If you have a 30HP engine and 20 HP screw the effective horsepower for the boat will be 20 HP. All the other engine activity just burns fuel.

Pitch of the screw is key as an over pitched screw will result in too much load on the engine and not allow it to get close to the maximum RPM of the engine. The engine is working too hard, but not pushing to attain the most speed. If your engine goes right up to maximum RPM when the throttle is pushed forward, the screw is under pitched as the engine does not have to work too hard. The boat is still not moving at hull speed for an engine fully capable of getting to hull speed.

A boat should use the largest possible screw that can swing in the space available. However, the screw should have a clearance at 10% of its diameter to assure it does not flex into the boat. A screw that is too close to the hull will create turbulence at its tips and lose efficiency.

$$\text{Hull Speed} = \sqrt{\text{waterline length}} \times 4/3 \quad **$$

** Attainable at approximately 2HP/1000 LBS

Sunnyside needs at least 52 HP per rule and has a 66HP Yanmar.

A new option for sail boats that eliminates the drag when the engine is not running and you are sailing is the Maxi Prop. Maxi Props are cool for sailboats, but expensive. The screw when rotated by the engine opens to a specified pitch. When sailing, and the engine is not turning, the screw collapses and lies flat with the water stream.

Engine RPM

When motoring, max RPM is not necessarily the best point. While the engine will probably run forever at that speed, you should monitor your speed and find the point that is good speed with less noise, minimal wake, and where adding RPM adds little speed.

Starting

Diesel engines start differently depending on the type of engine. Some boats have "glow plugs" that must be turned on for a while to heat up the engine before trying to start. My four cylinders Yanmar is kind of like a gas engine, turn the key and start the engine. However my 3 cylinder Yanmar generator engine starts much harder, like it is always cold.

Be sure and read your manual to see what is recommended for your engine. They are all a bit different. Some engines have compression relief valves to eliminate compression before starting. This results in it being easier to start those engines. Some engines may have a choke valve that operates like a choke on a gasoline engine. The thing I like about the Yanmar engine is you just turn the key and it starts, push the button and it stops. It is truly the KISS principle (Keep It Simple, Stupid).

Make sure you have a operations, maintenance, and parts manual for all engines on board your boat. You will need them unless you have lots of bucks to hire someone every time the engine does something weird.

Trouble Shooting Engine

Problem: Engine stops after going through rough water
1. Try to restart engine.
2. If it starts, check vacuum gauge if available. (If not, install one.)
3. If it will not start, check the fuel filter as it is probably clogged.
4. Switch to backup filter if available. (If not possible, install one later.)

5. Change clogged filter.

Problem: Engine will not start.
1. Open one of the injector lines at the engine. If a small amount of fuel spits out, you have fuel.
2. If no fuel spits out, open the bleeder valve ahead of the injection pump.
3. Manually or electrically pump untill air comes out (without engine turning).
4. If no fuel, rotate engine ½ turn and try to bleed again

Note: Injection pump only runs with engine. If fuel available at input, should come out the injector line.

➢ Lift Pumps almost never fail.

➢ Must Bleed when Engine Filter Changed. Installing a fuel pump will greatly aid this process and in most cases eliminate all the bleeding of lines when you change the engine fuel filters.

➢ If you use a Racor fuel filter you may never have to change the engine fuel filter as the Racor filter is a much finer mesh filter and will remove everything, including water, prior to the fuel getting to the engine filter.

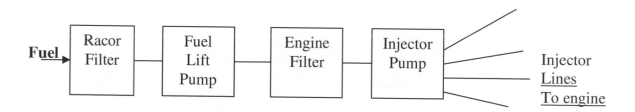

Chapter 5 – Electrical Systems

The DC System

The heart of your sailboat is really your house battery. It provides the basic energy source for your boat to run your systems, instruments, lights etc. Some folks also use 12V appliances such as microwaves, coffee pots, blenders etc.

The batteries on your boat should be divided up into two classes; house and starting. They have two distinctive functions that are very much different and, as a result, they require different types of batteries for each type of supply.

There are many types of batteries and many levels of cost for batteries. Typical marine batteries include: Lead Acid, Gel cell, and Absorbed Glass Mat (AGM.) There are other more expensive types, but the above three are usually available at most marine supply locations. A key difference in the batteries is that the voltages are not exactly the same on the different types as well as the charging rates can be different.

AGM seems to be the most expensive and they are the most forgiving when charging or discharging. You can charge them fast and hard. AGM batteries take vibration well as the electrolyte is held in a fiberglass matt. They may be turned upside down without spilling as they use a glass mat that absorbs the acid solution. This is different from the liquid in the lead acid batteries.

Gel Cells like to be treated tenderly when charging, but similar to the AGM they have no liquid to spill. Gel Cells cost a lot more than lead acid batteries and the only real plus I know is they do not spill when turned over as the electrolyte is in a gel form. Charging will require some modifications to your alternator to limit the charge rate for these batteries.

The lead acid battery is just like that in most cars or trucks. They have water mixed with acid surrounding the lead plates in each cell. Lead acid also come in sealed units so you do not have to mess with water. Friends have claimed that sealed lead acid last as long as the warranty. That may be true, but if you keep them charged and do not draw large amounts of current, they seem to last a long enough. The winter cold can kill all batteries if you do not keep a trickle charge on them. The liquid will spill out of these batteries if not kept upright.

While it is possible to use different batteries for starting and house, I would recommend you consider using the same type for both applications to make charging simpler. The issue becomes how to charge different types of batteries with the same source. It can be done, but just adds to the complexity of your system. There are several types of lead acid batteries based on use. The thickness of the plates determines how the battery should be used.

Starting Batteries - Starting batteries require a significant amount of short term current to supply the extensive current required by the starting motor. Fortunately this is a short term load and then the engine charges the battery backup when it is running.

Other high current things can run from this battery as well. However it is important that you connect only things that make sense as you want to make sure your starting battery is charged when you want to start the engine. One example of something that makes sense is the anchor windless. The reason it makes sense is you normally only operate the windless when the engine is running and charging the batteries. I also added my bow thruster on my starting battery for the same reason.

I standardized on lead acid batteries for reasons to be explained in the next section on the house batteries. When purchasing the starting battery there is little difference between ratings. For example, an 800 MCA battery costs just slightly less than a 1000 MCA battery. So for about $100 you can get a very good lead acid staring battery that will support your windless and bow thruster if you have one.

Don't put the inverter on the starting battery though. It will drain your starting battery to nothing. As you may remember from an earlier section, the inverter can use over 80 Amps for extended periods and then how would you start the engine?

House Batteries – The house batteries are typically a very large bank of batteries. Most cruisers have no less than 400 amp-hours of batteries. There is always a compromise with space, charging capability and need. Based on the items you have to run off the house battery, you can determine what size the house battery needs to be. House batteries should be deep cycle batteries to assure you get the maximum re-charge cycles and if needed, reserve energy is still available below the half power point.

The most important battery rating used to determine battery capacity is the Amp-Hour rating. This rating specifies that the battery will supply X number of amps for a period of Y hours at a certain rate. For a 200 amp-hour battery if you draw an average of 10 amps, the battery will be completely dead after 20 hours. If you run the battery to dead it will not provide 20 hours the next time. As a result, the battery really only should be used to supply about 100 amp-hours, assuming you are looking for the longest life possible out of your batteries.

A table I put together for my vessel to help determine the size required for my batteries and estimate time between charges is below and included on the CD for your use as an example. The file name is: "Battery Requirements"

DC Electricity Usage Calculator

Group	Device		Amps	Number in Use	Use Hours / Sub Total	Amp-hours
Communications					10.8	
	VHF Cockpit Xmit		6.00			0.00
	VHF Cockpit Receive		0.30		24.0	7.20
	VHF Nav Xmit		5.40			0.00
	VHF Nav Receive		0.70			0.00
	VHF Transfer Switch		0.03		24.0	0.72
	PA Amp		0.24		0.0	0.00
	HF Transmit		3.00			0.00
	HF Receive		1.40		2.0	2.80
	Charge Portable		0.50		0.2	0.10
						0.00
Navigation					46.6	
	Cockpit Breaker		0.26		24.0	6.17
	- Instruments					0.00
	- GPS					0.00
	Chart Plotter		0.63		24.0	15.19
	Handheld GPS		0.06			0.00
	Laptop		2.00			0.00
	Loran		0.55			0.00
	Radar transmit		3.00		4.0	12.00
	Radar Standby		2.20			0.00
						0.00
	Auto Pilot		1.10		12.0	13.20
	Fog Horn Timer		0.03			0.00
						0.00
						0.00
Navigation Lighting					17.9	
	Running Lights		2.24		8.0	17.92
	Mast Head Light		2.24			0.00
	Anchor Light		1.38			0.00
						0.00
Other Lights					0.0	
	Spreader Lights		5.07			0.00
	Cockpit Light					0.00
	Hand Spot Light					0.00
	Bow Light		3.65			0.00

Category	Item	Amps	Qty	Hours	Amp-hours
	Stern Light	2.68			
					0.00
Pumps				5.9	
	Fresh Water	7.00		0.2	1.40
	Bilge	8.30		0.5	4.15
	Fuel	0.60			0.00
	Shower sump Pump	3.00		0.1	0.30
					0.00
Galley				0.0	
	DC Refrigerator	6.00		0.0	0.00
	Propane Valve			2.0	0.00
					0.00
General Lighting				15.6	
	Incandescent Spots	1.80	1	3.0	5.40
	Fluorescent	1.70	2	3.0	10.20
					0.00
					0.00
Miscellaneous				30.0	
	Anchor Windlass	80.00			0.00
	Horn	5.00		6.0	30.00
	Inverter/ 500 W	45.00	0.0	0.0	0.00
	AM/FM Radio	1.00			0.00
	AM/FM Radio w Tape				0.00
	CD Player SW	0.00		24.0	0.00
	CD Player	0.80			0.00
	DVD	4.00			0.00
	TV on Inverter	9.00			0.00
					0.00
					0.00
					0.00
					0.00
					0.00
Battery Requirements	Discharge to 66%				**380.26**

The above spreadsheet is programmed so that if you turn the item on, it is added to the calculation. It can be used for sizing and estimating the next charge time.

After you determine the quantity of amp-hours you need, then you can size your batteries, charging systems etc. The more batteries installed and the higher usage (load) will result in more charges and/or longer charging periods.

Charging your batteries – Batteries are charged by increasing the voltage above the discharge level which forces current back into the battery. When you purchase batteries, one of the ratings is how many times you can re-charge the battery during the life of the battery. Actually that is the end of life of the battery. The life can end early if cells get shorted or too much crud is collected on the plates. The crud acts as insulation and keeps the cells from being charged or discharged.

To get to the most number of charge - discharge cycles, you must make sure the batteries are charged properly and that you charge before they have discharged too far. Again, for lead acid batteries they should not be discharged more than half power before re-charging.

Something to check out is a graph of your battery's voltage at which you are starting the charge vs. number of charges possible. As you allow a battery to discharge excessively, you are significantly reducing the number of times you can re-charge the battery. Charge early and your battery will last much longer.

For example: For a 200 Amp hour battery should only be allowed to discharge to half power of 100 Amp-hours. That is approximately a terminal voltage of approximately 12.2 volts with no load on the battery. So when looking at your house voltmeter and the reading is 12.2 volts, while not supplying a significant current, the battery is at half power. Of course when you turn the microwave on via connection to your inverter, it may result in a significant dip well below the 12.2 volts. This is as a result of the high current being sucked out of the battery through the battery's internal resistance. The internal resistance will drop the voltage available at the terminal until the high current drain is terminated.

Charging Batteries

Four stages of charging batteries include the Bulk, Absorption, Float, and Equalizing charge.

Ask the dealer for a graph of your battery's voltage at which you are starting the charge vs. number of charges possible. As you allow a battery to discharge excessively, you are reducing the number of times you can re-charge the battery. Charge early and your battery will last longer. For example, with a heavy current draw, charging your batteries twice a day instead of once a day when the battery is almost dead will extend the life of the batteries.

Bulk Charge – Charger voltage is raised to between 14.0V and 14.6V and held there to force the maximum current back into the battery. The time the charge will remain in the bulk rate is dependent on the battery's charge level at the time of initiating the charge and the charger's programming. A constant voltage is maintained.

Absorption Charge – The voltage is decreased some from the bulk charge level. A constant current flow back into the battery is maintained until the battery is fully charged.

Float Charge – The float charge is a maintenance type charge. Float charge keeps the battery level constant with a slight trickle charge back to the battery. Should a demand for more energy arise, the charger will generally try to provide the additional current and or make up the battery's loss of energy after the energy draw has completed.

Equalizing Charge – The equalizing charge is used to nock off the crud built on the battery plates so that all cells provide an equal amount of the energy supplied by the battery. This is accomplished by raising the charging voltage to a value higher than a normal bulk charge so that the sulphates that collected on the plates get knocked off. When doing an equalization charge, you must check the electrolyte in each cell and continue the charge until the specific gravity level is approximately equal in all cells. The specific gravity of each cell should be within the range of 1250 to 1300 if the cells are still good.

Charging from Shore Power – There are many good 110 VAC chargers available on the market. Be sure you have a 4 stage charger and not just a bulk charger as the four stage charger will not only maintain your batteries in the top condition, but when you are at the dock connected to 110VAC, it will supply all 12VDC power requirements without charging and discharging the batteries. charger having 4 stages will include the equalizing charge to again extend the life your batteries and make sure they do not discharge each other.

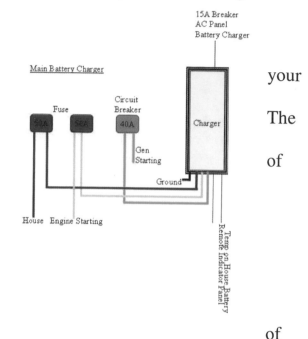

your

The

of

of

Charging from your Engine – There are several types of alternators with externally controlling regulators. Like your shore power connection, it is important that the regulator provide at least the first 3 stages charging. The alternator should have the capability of at least ¼ the current of the total battery Amp-hours. For example, a 400 Amp-Hour battery should have at least a 100 amp alternator on your engine.

Equalization charges may also be done from an engine alternator, but this is not the best approach as it burns fuel. Doing an equalization charge at sea can be dangerous as you should remove the caps on the batteries to allow for hydrogen gas to bubble out and also to let you measure the electrolyte to know when the charge is complete.

Charging from your Generator – Most cruising boats will also have a generator on board. Since the generator's fuel consumption is less than the engine, you may want to set up to utilize your generator as your charging source.

As a side benefit, running the generator can also provide re-charging of an AC refrigeration system, making water, etc. As many of the modern day 110VAC chargers do not operate efficiently with a marine generator, installing a large alternator with an external 3 stage regulator on your generator is a good move. Using the generator instead of your main engine to re-charge all your boats systems can extend your fuel range when you have wind in your sails.

Wind generator Charging – There are many good wind generators available on the market today and they get better and quieter every year. Some make more noise than others. Since we play in the wind, a wind generator can again extend your range and the times between charges.

Using the Sun to Charge Batteries – Solar cells are another source of increasing your time between charges. There are many different solar cells available today at many different pricing levels. You must select the cells that provide the energy you need in the space you have to install them. We installed a stern Arch on Sunnyside to add two 130W cells. We also installed two 130 watt cells on the hard top we installed. Hopefully that will provide adequate energy to allow my wife to dry her hair.

Keeping the batteries charged to provide energy on your boat is a key factor for cruising. It is important that you review your system's electrical requirements and then size your batteries and charging systems to get to the places to which you want to sail. If electrical is not something you know about, find another sailor that knows electrical and get some help.

AC Systems

The AC systems on modern cruising boats resemble those in your home. Microwaves, coffee pots, and even blenders to make margaritas can be found on cruising boats today.

To power these appliances, a boat has a separate AC panel and wiring to what appear to be regular home style outlets. Behind the scenes you will find some major differences in house wiring and boat wiring.

Outlets – First and most important, all the wire is not solid like in your home. All marine wire is stranded wire and the good stuff sold today is also tinned copper strands. That means the manufacturer of the wire has covered the copper wire with a material similar to solder to keep the wire from corroding.

While there are differences in how folks connect to the electrical outlets, my preferred method is to use crimp connectors. The crimp connectors are mechanically crimped into place providing a good mechanical connection. Then I solder them to keep the connection from corroding later. It is also recommended to use marine grade shrink tubing to seal off the end of the connector. The terminal lug is then connected to the AC outlet.

Breaker Panel – The breaker panel is frequently with the DC breaker panel and from the outside looks the same. It is important to remember though that the back side of the panel is very open and very hot with 120 Volts AC hanging out there. So take care when working on the panel.

The AC panel should also have a source switch. The source switch is used to direct shore power, inverter, or a generator to the AC panel.

Splitting Port and Starboard Bus – When I purchased Sunnyside the entire AC panel was routed through one of the two 30 amp

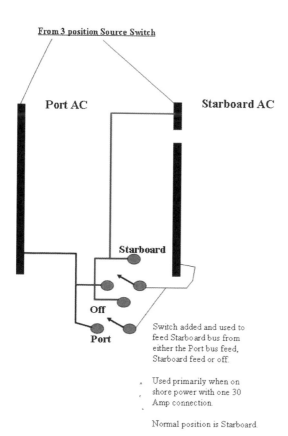

shore power cords. The second 30 amp power cord only provided power to the forward heat pump. By making a small change I shifted the bus so that one cord provides starboard power and the other cord provides port power. I also installed a switch that allows everything to run off the original single cord.

The key advantage in doing this was to modify the system such that if a failure to one side or power cord occurred; we at least still had the other side fully operational.

Splitting the system turned out to be a good thing. While I was traveling in January one year and my wife was on the boat alone, the current transformer burnt up and she was left with only port power. But she had power and could keep the boat warm. Splitting the system paid off as my wife was no where near as unhappy as she would have been with no power.

AC Generator

The diesel engine portion of your generator will function similarly to your main engine and require the same maintenance and preventative maintenance. Instead of rotating the boat's shaft and screw, the generator rotates a shaft connected to a rotating set of coils called the rotor within another set of stationary coils called the stator. There are a lot of variations of generators available within the market today. A few things your main engine and the generator engine have in common would include:

1. The oil needs to be changed just like the main engine.
2. The cooling system needs to be kept full of water and antifreeze.
3. The fuel filter needs to be clean and changed when excessive material is collected in the filter.
4. A water separating filter should be installed ahead of the fuel filter on the engine.
5. The vacuum level after the water separation filter should be monitored with a gauge.
6. The air intake filter should be clean.

As with your main engine the generator engine needs clean fuel and air to work. With the generator it needs to generate electricity as well to keep running.

When I bought Sunnyside the generator worked great. I did not run it for about 6 months and when I tried to start it, it would shut down as soon as I released the start button.

After considerable research, I found that the generator was not generating 120 VAC when the engine was running.

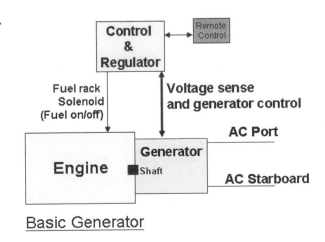

Basic Generator

Why my generator would not run

The Generator Basic Startup:

1. To start the generator, you press the start button.
2. The start button energizes the engine's starter and supplies battery voltage to the rotor winding via the brushes. At the same time a signal is sent to the fuel rack solenoid to provide fuel to the engine while the starting process is taking place.
3. A magnetic field is created in the rotor.
4. An 120 volts AC voltage is created at the output.
5. When the start switch is released, some of the output voltage is rectified and sent back to the rotor by the voltage regulator proportional to the amount of load required. The regulator also holds the solenoid, called the fuel rack solenoid, open to allow the engine to continue running.
6. For more things plugged into the generator's output, the more magnetic field will be required within the rotor to create more power out, so the current to the rotor is increased.
7. If there is no magnetic field being created, there is no output voltage.
8. The regulator turns off the voltage holding the fuel rack solenoid open. Like all good diesel engines, no fuel, no run.

On Sunnyside, by not using the generator for a long period, the brushes had corroded after sitting for 6 months.

After determining that the generator was not putting out 120V AC, I checked out the regulator and eventually pulled the hot water tank out so I could disassemble the generator. The brushes had grown green with corrosion. No voltage connection to the rotor resulted in no magnetic field and no output voltage.

I now start the generator and let it come to operating temperature at least twice a month. The generator has been working fine for the past four years.

In general it is a good practice to power up all your equipment at least on a monthly basis so that it works when you need it.

Another Tip that may save you pain:

On the Kohler generator on Sunnyside the starting circuit had a ten amp manual reset circuit breaker. The purpose of this device is to keep from overheating things when it takes too long to start the engine. When you have not used the generator for some time, it may take a while to start. Having to open the doors under the ladder to get to the reset every time I started the generator was a real pain.

I replaced the manual reset circuit breaker with a ten amp automatic reset breaker from a local auto parts company. Now when the engine is cold and I crank it too long the breaker still trips. But then by waiting a few seconds the breaker resets by itself No more crawling into the engine compartment and pushing that little red button.

Chapter 6 – Refrigeration

Refrigeration is a valuable side of comfort on a sail boat. There are many types of refrigeration units. Some are driven by the house batteries, some by 120VAC, and some by an engine or generator. There are also combinations of the three energy sources.

If you are buying a used boat, it probably already has some form of refrigeration have. Unless you are ready to spend some bucks, you are stuck with what you refrigeration system fails, you have new options that should consider all forms of providing the energy necessary to, as they say, keep the beer cool.

The refrigeration cycle is basically the same as the air conditioning cycle, except it is confined into a small space and is a lot colder. The way it works is simple:

1. A pump (called a compressor in refrigeration and air condition systems) extracts liquid Freon from a reservoir of low pressure liquid.
2. The compressor increases the pressure until it is a high pressure vapor.
3. The high pressure vapor is connected to the cooling plate by tubing.
4. When it arrives at the cooling plate the high pressure liquid is squirted into the cooling unit.
5. The spraying of the liquid results in the liquid boiling and flashing to a low pressure vapor. During that process the Freon absorbs all the heat within the cooling coils and is sent back to the reservoir.
6. The gas is cooled along the way and returns to a low pressure liquid state.
7. The low pressure liquid is again available for the compressor to start the cycle all over.

There are many ways to cool the liquid. At home a fan blows air across the cooling coils. Some boat systems use the same method.

Since we are surrounded with water on a boat, a more efficient system to cool the fluid on a boat is to use sea water. The sea water is circulated through a heat exchanger with the hot vapor running in the other adjacent tubing. The heat exchanger cools the gas and the Freon goes back to a cool liquid.

The maintenance issues with refrigeration:

1. The cooling unit leaks Freon to an insufficient level that causes it to provide poor cooling. Just like in your automobile when the Freon is low the air conditioning unit does not provide the cooling effect. If the unit is old, a re-charge may make it work. If the leak is too big, you need to find and repair the leak.
2. Compressor burns out. The compressor is the pump that creates the high pressure Freon gas. As the compressor has moving parts, it can also be a good source for leaking Freon.
3. Self inflicted failures: Some folks have admitted to poking a hole in the cooling unit when trying to scrape the ice off. This self inflicted pain is very costly, but can be used as an excuse to buy a new refrigeration system. For this problem, the solution is obvious. However, the cost can be high. I recommend letting your refrigeration and or deep freeze thaw a bit to eliminate the chiseling. A tip. Spray some Pam on the cooling unit before you turn it on and the ice will fall off in less time without scraping. Use a plastic scraper made for windshields on cars to remove the ice.

Another source for trouble can also be a water pump for the cooling water used to cool the Freon. On Sunnyside we have a 120VAC refrigeration unit that supplies Freon to a deepfreeze and a refrigerator. The returned Freon vapor is cooled with the water that is pumped through the refrigeration system. If the water is not supplied, the gas will not cool and return to the liquid state.

The pump has a strainer on it that needs to be cleaned and there is a hull valve that needs to be opened to make it all work. Keep the strainer clean and the valve open when the refrigerator is on. The water may also be used to cool the pump. If you forget to open the valve you may burn up the pump. (When I burnt my pump motor up on the air conditioning unit, it was pricey.)

Chapter 7 – The Head

While working on your heads can be a crappy job, they need some tender loving care just like the other systems on your boat. If you have purchased a used sailboat, the head(s) probably need attention. Put yourself in the past owner's place. Would you fix up the head if you were planning on selling your boat?

One main advantage freshwater over salt water flushing heads has beyond the better smell is that salt water and urine for almost a concrete in the hoses if not the line is not completely flushed of urine. For a manual flushing head we normally flush the urine down and then flush the salt water through the head for 20 pumps.

We recently replace one of our manual pumping heads with an electric head and I designed and built a timer to cause the head to flush for adjustable to 20 or 30 seconds with one push of the button. It has been a great upgrade to make the wife happier as 20-30 pumps was not in her vocabulary.

The head may have only a couple of valves or many as in the attached drawing. The valve V1 allows for the head to be dumped directly into the holding tank. V2 would dump the head overboard which would be against the law except when off shore at least 12 miles. The Coast Guard requires V2 to be locked or at a minimum <u>locked closed</u> unless off shore 12 miles.

V3 is used to pump the tank overboard when off shore. This valve should also be <u>locked closed</u> unless off shore.

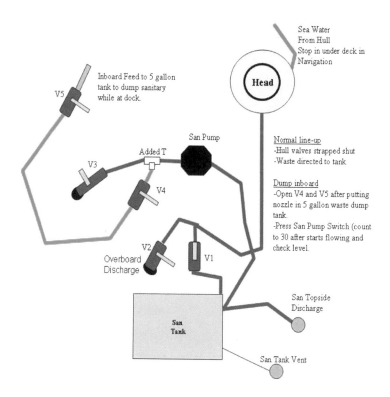

The normal method of getting rid of the waste would be to discharge the waste at a pump out station, frequently found at marinas and state owned docks.

Pump out stations usually provide a rubber hose connection to shove into the topside pump out connection. The pump out station takes suction on the tank and removes the waste. (Make sure your vent is clear so you are not drawing a vacuum on the tank, or the tank may collapse.)

As an alternative to a pump out station, I installed a Y connector on the overboard pumping line and added a hose connection through V 4 and V5 to allow pumping into a 5 gallon plastic tank. I use a plastic fuel tank marked waste when I am at the dock for long periods.

Since I was on my boat almost every weekend doing projects and I need crew to get the boat to the pump out station and back, this was a good alternative. Little smelly, but saves a lot of fuel and hassle with no crew in the winter.

Operational Skills
Chapter 8 – Docking

One of the skills that can be challenging when you start boating in a large boat is leaving and entering the dock. My first boat was a 25 foot I/O power boat. It was easy to park. When you turned the wheel, the screw (prop in the civilian world) turned and you went that way. Same when backing, it always responded to the wheel. Not with a single screw and a single rudder.

If you have a small boat it is easy to man-handle, sorry people-handle, it into the dock or out. However, when I purchased Sunnyside, a 45 foot - thirteen ton sailboat, the first thing I found out was that turning the wheel did not necessarily make things happen. Clearly, it worked fine when I was moving forward at a reasonable rate, but backing up and parking were a challenge. The wind and current caused Sunnyside to go where they wanted her to go instead of what I was suggesting by turning the wheel. After some significant damage to Sunnyside and a few other boats, I did the two following things.

First I had a bow thruster installed. After hitting the same boat twice it seemed to be the right thing and the thruster cost less than the damage I did the last time we collided. Since insurance costs so much anyway, the last thing I wanted to do was turn in a claim and have the rates go up. The bow thruster helps a lot, but it is only part of the answer. With a bow thruster installed, you can get in just as much trouble on a windy day or when there are high currents if you do not understand how to drive your boat.

Secondly and the most important step: I bought a book on handling a single prop, single rudder boat for about $25. What an eye opener. After reading the book, I made sense out of what was really happening. It now made sense, but required practice. I would highly recommend that everyone purchase a book on handling a single prop, single rudder boat.

To give you an idea of what things you need to be thinking about, I have included some of the key aspects of handling a single prop, single rudder boat.

1. **Prop walk** - When you back up your boat the rotation of the prop will cause you to turn to one side or the other. If you have a right handed prop your boat will move toward the port (the aft end will turn to the left). For a left handed prop it will walk the other way. Check to see which one you have in open water (away from the dock so nothing gets damaged) wheel to the amid-ship (center position) and put the engine in reverse. Determine if the boat is rotating to port or starboard when you back. That is the prop walk direction you must account for when backing.

   This is very valuable information as when you are leaving the dock, if you are tied up to the port side of your boat (a port tie), and you start backing out your boat will push into the dock. This could be the first damage to your new boat. The dock may create a great looking rub mark along the side of the boat at dock level as it pushes tighter and tighter against the dock. Without reading the rest of this section, even a fender will help eliminate this problem, but the dock may scrape up the new fender.

   If you have a starboard tie, the prop walk could help you get out without damage, but docking may be a bit more difficult.

2. **Using the Rudder as a Thruster** - You can compensate for prop walk by using your prop and rudder as a stern thruster. The boat moves according to how the water is pushed past the rudder. That is why when you turn the rudder at slow speeds, nothing may happen as water is not passing by the rudder with enough force to move the boat. Don't forget the keel is saying go straight, and the prop may be trying to walk the boat.

   If you rotate the wheel so that your boat would steer right (to Starboard) and give a quick blast on the prop forward then an equal blast aft the boat's stern will move to the port. This happens because the forward surge causes a jet stream to pass the rudder pushing the boat to port. The surge aft does not go by the rudder so no port or starboard direction occurs. The surge aft only keeps the boat from driving forward from the shot forward we did.

   One of the reasons this works well is that with a large boat, it takes a lot of energy to get it going forward or aft. So if done properly, you will not move too far forward or aft. You will, however, move side to side. This rudder/engine thruster action will have significantly more power than the effect from the prop walk if done properly.

If you need to move sideways to keep from scraping the boat, give it a thruster shot with your rudder and prop. Turn the wheel hard right to go left and hard left to go right.

Before you try this at the dock, give it a shot in open water so you can get comfortable with how big a shot of power you need to do in both the forward and reverse directions. Using the rudder as a thruster is a very powerful skill to have in your boating skill bag. It can mean the difference in damage or no damage.

3. **Lines and Fenders to keep you safe** – When you are at a dock and wanting to leave, but the current and or the wind is holding you close to the dock, plan your exit using fenders and lines.

The ability to use power against a spring line rotate your boat is simple, but requires a bit of thought and practice. For example a spring tied aft, as in the example, and your engine in 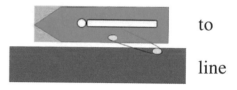 to line forward will result in the boat rotating to the right. Be sure and put a fender or two on the stern section though as it could result in a scrape. However if the wind is blowing in from the starboard side holding you against the dock, this may be the only way to get away.

If you wanted to rotate the stern out first you could extend the spring line forward and then backing the boat will cause the stern to come out first. Dependent on the wind and boat size, you might want to capture the loose end under your cleat so it does not pull out of your hands.

There are a lot of techniques using lines and fenders to move the boat away from a dock safely and most of them are common sense if you think about the situation before trying to get underway. It is worthwhile to learn more

Not Cool

about this skill and try it a few times to see how your boat responds.

4. **Tying up your boat at the dock** – I have seen many interesting ways of tying up a boat at a dock. For a small boat it may not be that important as you can keep it somewhat safe with a lot of fenders.

The one I really like as I walk down the dock is the bow line stern line and amidships line. This does not work well on any boat, but the little guys get away with it because they are little. What will happen is when the wind blows or the current is from the aft, the boat will move forward and bounce against the dock or fenders. When the opposite is true the boat will float aft.

When you have a boat displacing 13 tons it is important that you have it tied such that it does not bounce off the dock or even your fenders while you are gone. If a breeze kicks up and starts to move a multi-ton boat, there is a lot of momentum developed before it stops at the end of the lines. This puts a lot of stress on the lines and eventually they will break.

A common method uses an amidships cleat on the boat to restrict the forward and aft movement with lines running to forward and aft dock cleats. Frequently the bow and stern lines are long enough to use for both lines.

That is after tying off the bow to the forward dock cleat (restricting the amount of movement the boat can move away from the dock) the line is then brought back to the amidships cleat on the boat. The same technique may be used for the stern line. This technique is far superior to the above technique. When the boat does not have an amidships cleat the line is frequently tied to rigging.

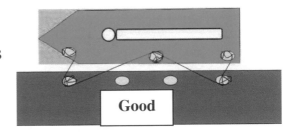

There are a lot of correct ways, but it is important to have good bow and stern lines to limit the amount of movement away from the dock. Properly installed spring lines will result in minimizing the fore and

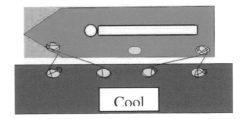

aft movement. I like to tie from the bow to a dock cleat near the center of the boat. This limits the forward and aft movement as well as limits the rotation of the boat. Bottom line, the boat sits still.

The example I have shown is how I tie Sunnyside and my preferred method. I know it works as I have a manually aligned TV satellite dish on the stern of the boat. Even when waves come in, the boat stays stable enough to watch TV.

I have also seen spring lines tied to the amidships cleats on the boat to the forward and aft dock cleats, but that would only control the forward and aft movement and not the twisting movement. For example, my TV would never work…..

5. **Tying off a line** – There are many examples of how not to tie to a cleat at every marina. While it is not difficult, it seems to be a mystery to many and the only thing that may result is your boat getting free while you are gone. A few practice runs on a cleat may save you the embarrassment of the missing boat when you return to the marina.

1. First of all take a loop around the cleat.

2. Then loop over the end of the cleat.

3. Then simply tie a half hitch on the other end.

4. If possible bring your lines back to the boat to tie them off as it gives you two lines of strength and allows for an easy departure while everyone is on board.

5. If you keep your lines on the dock, lay them out flat so others do not trip over them. A coil works great and looks kind of cool.

6. **Catching the boat when docking –** When coming into a dock it is important to control the situation. All of your lines should be ready as well as the fenders in place. The most important place for the Skipper of the vessel is at the helm. That means the skipper needs to pre-train the crew to do the appropriate things when docking. It may be different for each boat depending on how the boat is rigged, but without a bow thruster, a line from the amidships cleat brought to the stern tie cleat on the dock will tend to bring the boat into the dock and stop it at the same time. If you do not have an amidships cleat, use a shroud or rail to tie the boat up. Be careful though, tying to a shroud may cut the rope and tying to a rail may bend the rail. It might be best to install a big cleat with back up plates.

Bring the boat in slowly and steer so that your crew does not have to jump to the dock. Having someone sprain or break a leg coming in makes for a bad day and most importantly there may be no one else to help tie up your boat. So take it slow and tell them not to get too eager to get ashore.

The second scary mistake I have seen people doing all the time is trying to catch the boat using their strength. Even the best people I know cannot hold back 13 tons headed for the dock. Make sure they get a line under a cleat as soon as possible as the cleat will provide friction and leverage to keep the boat from going with the wind.

Another mistake often made is relying on strangers to stop your boat. Untrained in the techniques that work for your boat, bystanders trying to help can result in damage to your boat and/or to themselves. On Sunnyside I have had only one close call this past year. The close call was as a direct result of a cute little girl who wanted to help on my stopping line. Unfortunately, my crew member was such a nice person and failed to demand that she turn over the line to him. We stopped OK, but she left so much line out that the wind blew us sideways and bumped the vessel along the outboard side. Fortunately there was no damage.

Always put your most trained crew member on the stopping line!

I recently made up an official stopping line for my normal dock. It has a small loop on one end and a larger loop on the other end. When coming in the small loop is attached to the amidships cleat and the larger loop is extended to the dock using a boat hook. As the boat arrives at the dock the large loop is placed over the after dock cleat. The line is just long enough so that the boat will not go past the normal docked position. As the line tightens the boat is pulled to the dock and the crew can step off of a stopped boat adjacent to the dock and tie up the lines. No one is required to jump, run, or use unknown people at the dock. It makes for a safe landing.

A similar approach might be possible even on the East Coast where boats are frequently tied to pilings. The creative sailor might rig up a simple method of clipping onto an after piling line as the bow of the boat passes.

Chapter 9 – Anchoring

Anchoring can be fun. When we had a small power boat anchoring was throwing the big heavy thing on the bow over the side. One night I woke up and felt like we were moving. I sprang out of bed and sure enough the wind was blowing us sideways. We were being blown toward, what looked like in the middle of the night, the Queen Mary. I yelled for my wife Pat to come topside and hold off the stern while I lit off the blowers long enough to rid the engine compartment of fumes. (An explosion could have really made it a bad night.)

Pat ran up in her bath robe and started holding us off the Queen Mary. Someone from way up above looking down asked, "you need any help down there". Interestingly enough we both think he was more interested in copping a look at Pat's open shorty robe as the robe was her entire wardrobe on that hot night.

After that little after midnight challenge, I started checking out the books on how to anchor properly.

Anchoring properly is not rocket science, but can easily end up in running with the wind. There are many ways to add staying power to your anchoring situation. This book only discusses the basics of anchoring so you don't have to expose some of your wife's classified body parts in the middle of the night.

The Keys to Basic Anchoring

There are many styles of setting an anchor. Some of them even work. I now realize you need to do more than touch the bottom with your anchor. (That is what got us in trouble on the old power boat.) You will find books and magazine articles that do a great job of detailing different schemes, anchor types and rode types for anchoring.

Get enough rode (anchor line) out. For day parking you should let out anchor line equal to five times the depth of the water. Overnight you should let out at least seven times the depth of the deepest water during the period to be anchored. In a storm, put it all out.

Here is the process that seems to work.

1. In an area where the water level changes either as a result of tide changes or dams on a river, it is important to look at the entire period you will be at anchor. Check the tide tables for the maximum depth the water will be at during your stay.

   It is more difficult dealing with rivers with dams as you may not know when the dam might dump a lot of water raising the water level in the middle of the night or shutting off the flow. If you do not have past experiences in an area, don't be afraid to ask locals.

2. You must also consider others that are in the same anchorage area. If you are in twelve feet of water and have 84 feet of chain out that means you could make a circle around your anchor of 168 feet. Make sure that you are not going to rotate to a new position and run over your neighbor's boat or anchor line. The last <u>vessel in has</u> the responsibility to make sure that it does not create a problem. Remember there may be at least one boat that does not turn in the wind as a result of a stern anchor. Figuring this out is always easier in the day light if possible. For additional safety, add extra space when arriving at night.

3. Select a center point to drop the anchor at approximately the middle of the potential rotation of the boat if the wind and/or tide changes.

4. Position yourself at that center point with the wind and/or current and/or engine pushing your vessel aft.

5. Start letting out the anchor rode and let the boat drift/drive backward with the engine in reverse set at idle. (If you plan to set a GPS alarm, do it now so that you can adjust for your circle around the anchor point.)

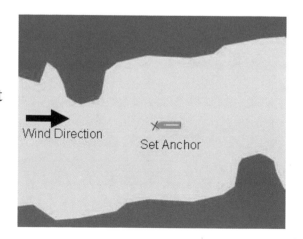

Wind Direction   Set Anchor

6. When you get the calculated rode let out, increase you engine speed slightly to set the anchor hard.

7. Monitor your GPS on the smallest scale to assure the anchor is holding.

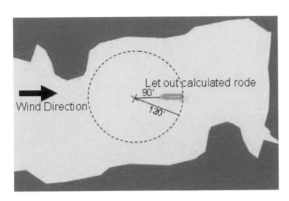

8. After letting out the required rode, I usually place a waypoint at that location to see how if I am drifting. I watch the GPS on the most detailed scale for a while to see if I am moving.

9. While you are awake and can monitor the possibility of dragging your anchor, it is a good practice to let out anchor rode (rope or chain) equal to five times the maximum depth of the water. If you are going to stay over night, multiply the maximum depth for the whole period times seven and let out that much rode.

10. Re-check your location for a change in tide, wind, or current direction. Place another waypoint at the shifted location as another reference point.

11. Set the anchor watch on your depth finder so that if the depth increases or decreases beyond certain thresholds, an alarm will go off to alert you. Some GPS units also have an anchor watch function that can be set to alarm if you start drifting down the creek or out to sea.

12. You can easily calculate the thresholds by looking at the terrain around you on a chart. Don't forget the amount of rode you have out will determine your anchor's holding power.

Occasionally you will see folks running a line to the shore from the stern or putting out a stern anchor. This does a couple of things. One it can keep tension on the anchor so it does not pull free. Secondly it will keep you from swinging with the wind or current and hitting another boat that is anchored near you. If the one of the anchors looses ground, it can be a mess trying to untangle the two sets of anchor rode.

Chapter 10 – Navigation

Many boaters think that navigation is; knowing where you are, where you are going and being able to get there at approximately some time and date. While making holes in the ocean on a submarine, we were often challenged by two navigation challenges that shall be discussed in this chapter. Remember; contrary to popular belief, there are no windows on submarines, so it is all about navigation. A submarine does have a periscope that may be used for navigation when the submarine is at periscope depth. The Officer of the Deck can, as we use to say, take a little periscope liberty and if land is in site, get some bearings.

The two challenges of navigation: How do I get from Point A to Point B. (Where are we?) More importantly we need to know what other vessels might be near us and how to avoid them. (Who else is out there?) While you're new sailboat may not be limited to a periscope to view the world through, when you get in a bank of fog, you will wish you had a magic periscope that can see the world around you. The most important part of navigation to me is "who else is out there?" Normally you will have a significantly longer period of time to determine where you are going than to get out of the way of a big freighter.

If you are not familiar with navigation, you should get a lot of training before venturing out into the ocean. There are no signs and it is easy to go in circles as everything looks the same when you cannot see land.

A few basic tips in fog and at night:

1. Make yourself visible – Get a radar reflector for your boat. They make your plastic or wood boat look like a real metal vessel. If you have a metal boat, your reflection should be better, but a radar reflector still would not hurt.
2. If in the fog, sound a horn every 1-2 minutes for 5 seconds if motoring and add a long and two short blasts if sailing.
3. Use your radar to look for other vessels.
4. Listen for other vessels' horns blowing and try to make sure you know where they are coming from. This is an all hands project for all persons who are in the cockpit.

5. Calculate a best guesstimate of when the other vessel will arrive nearest your location.

Who Else is Out There?

In the Navy we referred to other vessels as contacts. On a nuclear submarine, contact avoidance is critical at sea as well as when you are trying to get underway leaving a port. As a result, when I think of navigation I think first of moving so that I do not hit anything.

The best way to detect who else is out there is through proper use of your radar. Basic radar operation is covered in another section of this book.

There are some approximations you can use to get a gut feeling as to contacts traveling around you. You have to be especially careful during fog or on dark and dreary nights. Contact avoidance is especially important during all of those periods.

Examples: When big ships are coming into a restricted area such as a river or channel in the fog, they often report on VHF channel 16 that they are passing an entrance buoy number. Find that buoy on your chart so you can quickly determine if the contact will be a threat to your vessel. Basically you need to know if and/or when the contact will be close to you.

1. **Moving into a new River**
   Say you are moving into a traffic area and hear a ship is transiting a lane you intend to join in 10 minutes.

   Question: Where the ship will be when you enter the traffic lane?

   What I do is estimate the speed of the tanker at say 20 knots and 14 knots. That means the contact vessel will travel between 0.33 nautical miles in one minute (3.3 mile in ten minutes) and 0.23 nautical miles in one minute (2.3 miles in ten minutes). Quick calculations in the cockpit:

One Minute Distance =   speed/60
          @ 20 Knts   = 20/60
                            = 2/6 = 1/3
                            = 0.33 nautical miles in one minute
And   @ 14 Knts   = 14/60 = 7/30
                            = 0.23 nautical miles in one minute

Distance in a minute multiplied times the number of minutes till you expect to reach the point will give you an idea where the danger might exist. When roughing out the position don't forget that one minute of Latitude is approximately equal to one nautical mile. So the scale is always available on the chart for your use.

In 10 Minutes   = 0.23 X 10 = 2.3 nautical miles in ten minutes
In 10 Minutes   = 0.33 X 10 = 3.3 nautical miles in ten minutes

Based on the above calculations, the contact will cover between 2.3 and 3.3 nautical miles in the ten minutes that your vessel will take to get to the vessel meeting point.

Next take and plot out on your chart the distance 2.3 nautical miles and 3.3 nautical miles from the buoy, assuming the contact will be traveling within the traffic lane.

If the two points are within your range of entry you may want to do some of the following things to assure your safety.

1. Slow your vessel so that the contact will be sure to pass before your arrival at the meeting point.
2. Contact the contact vessel on VHF to verify the contact's actual speed.
3. Contact the contact vessel when you are within five minutes of the entry point to verify the contact's position.
4. Listen to the VHF for reports of the vessel passing other buoys while transiting the traffic lane.
5. Keep the radar running and verify the contact's position.
6. Remain outside the channel until the contact has clearly passed your entry point.

7. Remain outside the shipping channel until the fog has cleared sufficiently enough to allow a few miles of warning that a vessel is approaching.

Hopefully, the visibility will be a mile or more and you will be able to visually navigate around the contact. However, frequently that is not the case. As the skipper on your boat you are legally responsible for collision avoidance. Not wanting to swim in cold water is also a good reason to pay attention.

IMPORTANT: Always assume the other vessel(s) cannot see you visually or on their radar. This is the safest approach to making sure you survive the sea. That means that if you do everything that you can to affect collision avoidance, you should not have a collision. If the contact can see your vessel it will enhance your ability to keep your boats mast pointing up and you from not having to practice your swimming skills.

A few other rules of thumb, as engineers call them, would include a couple of numbers to have on top of your head when things start happening.

1. As above if we take the speed in knots times 2000 yards and then divide by 60 minutes we get the yards/minute. If we leave the speed off and multiply by 3 minutes we have a distance of 100 yards. Multiplying that times the speed of 6 knots yields 600 yards in 3 minutes. So in the cockpit you can get a feel for movement by multiplying the speed times 100 and the answer is in yards.
2. Using the above calculation if you are traveling at 5 knots, in 3 minutes you will travel 500 yards. Since 2000 yards is a mile it will take 4 intervals of 3 minutes, or 12 minutes to go a mile.
3. Another twist on this is the 10 minute mile. If you are traveling at 6 knots in 10 minutes you will travel one mile or 2000 yards. $(6/60 = 0.1nm) \times 10 = 1$ nm in ten minutes.

2. **Being Overtaken by a Ships**

Say you have a biggg ship coming up from behind you on the same track. A good question to ask is when will that ship be close to you? Going back to the speed calculations we did before, we can do some additional quick math and find out when we will have company at our location.

This time since the ship is traveling with us so we need to subtract our speed from the estimate speed of the other vessel. If we are doing 5 nautical miles per hour and we think they are doing 15, the other ship will be catching up to us at the rate of 10 nautical miles per hour. Simply put if they are ten miles behind us it will take an hour to catch up.

You may also want to calculate where you will be in an hour. That is five miles down the course you are on.

Try to keep it simple so you can do the numbers in your head. This is especially important when all you can see is fog.

3. **Meeting other vessels**
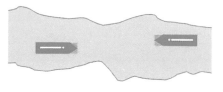
Say you have a biggg ship coming toward you. Again, when will the ship be close to you now? This is the same calculation as above except you now add your speed to the oncoming ship. That means it will be closing quickly.

Example: Assume your own sailboat is running at 5 knots and an oncoming ship is traveling at 15 knots. That means your closing speed to the other ship is 20 knots. From the calculations in 1 we see that 20 knots is a closing rate of 0.33 nautical miles per minute or in other words, every 3 minutes the ship will be a mile closer to you. Again keep it simple as you do not want to drag out your calculator every time you hear a big ship is coming.

Having these tricks in your sea bag can help you think fast when it is necessary.

Question: When will you meet the ship coming at you 1 nm away at 15 knots if you are going 5 knots toward the contact vessel.
Answer: 15+ 5 = 20 Knts/hour Or 2000 Yards In 3 minutes. 2000 Yards is 1nm so the answer is 3 minutes.

Question: It is 12:15 and we are making 6.5 knots to the good through the water to a point 4 miles away. What is the latest we will be at the point.

<u>Long hand solution</u>
- 4 miles X 2000 Yards = 8000 Yards
- 6.5 Knots X 2000/60 = 216.67 yards per minute
- 8000 yards / 216.67 = 36.92 minutes
- 12:15 + 36.92 minutes = 12:51.9 or 12:52

Short hand Answers: Using the 10 minute rule we know at 6 knots we will do a mile in 10 minutes so even if we slow a bit we can be there by 12:15 + (4 X 10) or by 12:55.

If we apply the 3 minute rule we will do 650 yards every 3 minutes. We have 4 miles X 2000 yards or 8000 yards to go. And 8000/650 is about 12 1/3. 12 1/3 intervals times 3 minutes is about 37 minutes for expected arrival.
We should arrive between 12:52 and 12:55.

For a sailor, the 12:55 would have been close enough for sailor time.

Play with it a bit and see how else you can apply the rules of thumb to keep from having to use a calculator in the cockpit.

Where Am I?

Latitude and Longitude Basics

A rule of thumb is that one minute of Latitude is equal to one nautical mile. One nautical mile is equal to 2000 yards or 6000 feet as opposed to the nice round statute mile number of 5,280 feet. So to estimate distance on a chart you can use the latitude scale for each minute of Latitude is approximately one nautical mile. Don't get mixed up though as Longitude is a quite different number. See the graph below. The graph shows how as the Longitude increases from 0 degrees to 90 degrees, North or South Pole, a minute of latitude slightly increases in distance. For longitude it is quite different as you can see. A minute of Longitude ranges from approximately one nautical mile at the equator but eventually goes to zero nautical miles at the north and south poles.

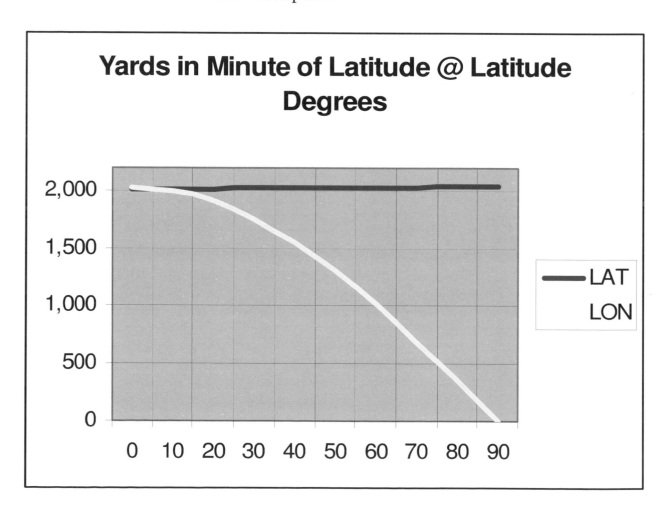

Finding your location is the main challenge of the sailor when there are big ships around that can hurt you or not. Unfortunately and fortunately we have GPS (GeoPolar Satellites). GPS is to navigation as the calculator is to calculations. When we used the slide rule to do complex calculations, we were always real close. Most importantly, you could not do a calculation without understanding the numbers you were dealing with.

The GPS gives us a very accurate calculation of our position, direction of travel and speed of travel. It is very important to know what to do in the event it is dark, there is fog, etc., and the GPS dies. The first time this happened to me I was only marginally prepared. Total darkness in a harbor for the first time can be real exciting.

A few guidelines to keep safe:

Obviously the safest way to stay out of trouble is to plot your position on a paper chart. Plot your course and calculate the set and drift based on the position fixes from the GPS. Then if the GPS dies, you just don't have a fix for a while.

Today's GPS technology is so good and the chart plotters add so much value that to my surprise, even the US Navy is moving toward paperless charts. It should not be forgotten the Navy will have redundant systems. The Navy's systems will also be expensive, professional type systems instead of the ones we get off the shelf at the local boat marine store.

Given that the average new sailors will probably depend heavily on their GPS instead of plotting on paper charts, the following recommendations may just help you stay out of trouble.

1. Have the paper charts on board and be familiar with them for the area you plan to travel.
2. Keep a log that identifies your GPS position, Speed Over Ground (SOG), Course Over Ground (COG), compass heading, and boat speed.
3. Take log readings as frequently as required to stay out of trouble if the GPS dies. While coastal sailing, I like to take readings every hour. My logic is I can get the data I have been gathering onto my charts within 15 minutes. I also would typically maintain my last compass heading. That course is

actually one that was compensated for set and drift since the GPS had you traveling directly to the next waypoint.

4. Know how to plot your position and a vector line that will represent the compass direction you are headed and your boat's speed as measured by your speed indicator.

5. Compare the vector line to the course you have been maintaining to remain on track as indicated by the GPS.

6. You should have an idea now what the set and drift were at the time you lost your GPS.

7. Eventually you will need more position fixes to update the set and drift.

For Coastal sailing, you can take bearings and or ranges to points of land, towers, etc. that are shown on your charts. The point at where the bearings cross is where you are. You can use you radar to obtain a range and bearing to a point which will yield a position. (Make sure you have verified the bearing as the antenna was mounted on your boat before getting bearing fixes. See the section on radar for more information on verifying bearing accuracy)

You can take two bearings or two ranges and identify where they cross on your chart to obtain a position. Since you are moving, be sure and record the time of the position fixes. These position fixes will not be as accurate as your GPS. Taking more position fixes and or ranges and bearings to other objects will increase your accuracy.

Two range and bearing fixes plotted together really provide two position fixes and can improve the accuracy of your fixes. They do need to be obtained quickly and close together with an accurate time they were taken for it to work best.

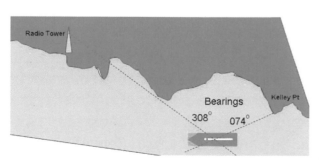

Another tool is a bearing finder. This can be a small handheld unit available at most boating stores or many marine binoculars come with a compass in it. The binoculars work really well as you can see your targeted point better than with a bearing finder. Taking two bearings, similar to radar positions, will provide a crossing. Taking three will give you a tighter position fix. Again, since you are not plotting immediately on the chart like your chart plotter, you need to get a good time so that when you are calculating set and drift it will be based on the time the position fix was obtained.

When you travel beyond the sight of land, there are no longer reference points from which to obtain position fixes. A hand held GPS, Loran, and a Sextant are good things to have on your sailboat for blue water travel.

Plotting fixes

Position fixes (FIX) obtained from a source identifies a specific point on earth. Different position location devices may have a wide range of accuracy. When we think of position location today, most of us think about the GPS. For mariners, the Loran 'C' has been a past source of determining where you are within the oceans and seas of the world for as long as I remember. Before Loran 'C' there was Loran 'A' which was even less accurate. Never the less, you could always make sure what ocean you were in from Loran 'A.'

Something to keep in mind is that the accuracy of a position fix ranges from differential GPS at within a few meters to Loran 'C', within 30-200 meters dependent on the location within the Loran 'C' group. When using a sextant to obtain a FIX, it is very dependent on accuracy of time and the operator's skill. It could be close or within a mile or so.

FIXes may be obtained from many sources. When using FIX devices that provide Latitude and Longitude directly such as a GPS or Loran it is a simple translation from the device to the chart. A FIX is always associated with a time. Unless you are tied to a dock, the time of the fix is critical. For GPS positions recorded on a plotter eliminates the importance of the FIX time. When using a sextant, it is very critical that you associate your readings with an exact time.

When plotting FIXes make sure you are plotting the proper format. Positions may be given in degrees, minutes and seconds or degrees, minutes and tenths of a minute by the same device. Charts may also use both methods. For example: 48° 30" 20'N and 122° 30" 37'W and 48° 30.33"N and 122° 30.62"W are approximately the same location on earth.

The conversion between minutes and seconds vs. minutes and tenths of seconds is simple. Like a clock there are 60 seconds in a minute so if you know the seconds just divide by 60 to find out how many tenths of minutes are in the position. Multiply tenths of minutes times 60 to obtain seconds.

◆ Going from Seconds to minutes in the above example of 20'

    20'/60 =.33333" or .33" for plotting.

◆ If you need to go from tenths of a minute to <u>seconds, such</u> as 0.5' then:

    0.5 minutes X 60seconds/Minute = 30 seconds

Now that you have a FIX with the time associated with it, you are now ready to plot it on your chart. Using dividers go to the edge of the chart and locate your position north/south or east/west. Locate a line of latitude or longitude as applicable that runs from the edge of the chart through the location where you think you are and within the reach of the dividers you are using.

With the dividers measure between the line you have selected and the latitude and then the longitude of the FIX. Plot the location where the latitude and longitude cross. You can use any symbol you want, but a triangle over the X you located works well. Note the time you obtained the FIX near the triangle. When noting the time it works best if you use a 24 hour clock so that there is no need to display a.m. and p.m. If you are transiting across an ocean the date should also be noted.

Plotting Speed vectors

A speed vector may be used for several things when sailing. A type of speed vector would be plotting out your expected location in an hour based on the speed you are going in the direction your compass says you are going. This would be a type of a speed vector.

A speed vector can also be a relative or true speed of another ship you see on your radar.

When plotting a speed vector on a chart, the plotting should also note the type of direction, either true or magnetic. For example, 148°M or 148°T

When you plot the vector the length is proportional to the speed or nautical miles per hour and the direction will be consistent with the chart's orientation. To plot the vector 15 nautical miles per hour in the direction of 148°M from the last FIX we took:

1. Measure 15 nautical miles on the latitude scale, 15 minutes.
2. Place your parallel ruler on the chart rose along the 148°M.
3. Walk the parallel ruler to the last FIX you plotted.
4. In the direction of the 148°M from the fix, mark the endpoint your dividers reached.
5. Draw a straight line along the ruler from the FIX to the endpoint location where you will be in an hour.
6. Label the vector 15Knts/148°M

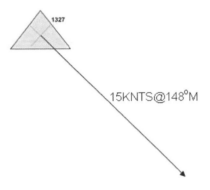

Even though a sailboat does not typically sail along at 15 Knots, it works at 5 Knots. You could also plot a 3 hour vector at the 5 Knots which would provide a vector 15 nautical miles long.

When plotting vectors against your own position, it is called dead reckoning. As time passes you should be someplace along the line, assuming you are maintaining the heading and speed through the water. Dead reckoning also assumes there is no current, no wind, and the instruments are accurate. In other words, when you get your next fix you will not be exactly where you thought you should be. Hopefully you will be close to the track. Set and drift, the correction to a dead reckoning course, will be discussed in the next section.

I use speed vectors to keep track of other vessels and figure out where I am going.

Plotting and using Set and Drift

When you drive your boat from point "A" to point "B", other earth's factors (current, wind direction and speed) will play into the actual direction you are traveling and how fast you are getting there. Using your traditional instruments such as speed through water and your compass to follow your course from point "A" to "B" will result in both speed and direction errors as the earth's factors move you around.

Basically, if I have a five knot current I am headed into and my boat speed through the water is 5 knots, I am going nowhere over the earth's surface. Likewise if we are going with the current, we will be traveling at 10 knots over the earth's surface. As you might expect, then a current of 5 knots coming on the beam of your boat will push you sideways while you are traveling forward at 5 knots.   If you are familiar with trigonometry you have already figured out that your speed forward (course over ground) is actually only about 3.5 knots at a course 45 degrees away from the heading of the boat.

Getting there with the basics

When plotting an initial course, we may not know what the earth's factors will do to us. Therefore we set a course for a compass heading and a speed we calculated to arrive at a certain time. We plot a course and speed vector for our destination. As we move along in

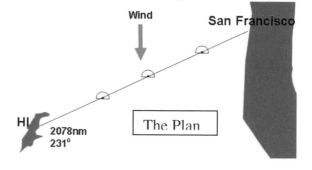

time we can plot our travel with a point and time that indicates where we think we are, based on speed and compass direction. This plot is referred to as the dead reckoning position. If you are traveling at 5 knots, every hour you should be 5 knots farther down your track line. The track line should run from the starting point to the end point. KISS

If there is no source to identify the actual location of the boat, such as Sextant, Loran or GPS, it may be possible to get close to our destination using only the compass and speed indicator. When we arrive at land it may be challenging to determine where we are in order to navigate using land points and a chart. If the destination were a long way away, hundreds of miles away or in the middle of the ocean, it would be nearly impossible to reach the destination without fix position information.

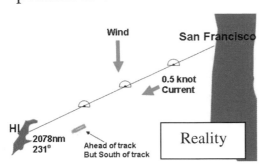

Unless you are cruising in a lake, bay or river it may be important to occasionally figure out where you are and how to change course to get to your destination. So as we move along our track it is important to occasionally get a position fix.

Obtain a fix and then plot it on your chart. The difference in where you think you are located (dead reckoning position) and the actual position based on the fix position is referred to as position error. Who would have thought?

The reason for calculating the set and drift is to allow you to modify your coarse and/or speed to correct for the earth's factors.

We need to look at two factors. <u>Drift</u> – moving through the water with no propulsion and Set – the direction of a current

Calculating Set and drift

Calculating the set and drift and the compensation for it can be accomplished in several ways. Since this is not intended to be a detailed course on navigation, but a method of doing quick calculations to make sure you get where you are going, the following provides a graphical (on the chart) approach to solving your navigation requirements. The following example illustrates two fixes that are twenty hours apart. Hopefully you will have several fixes each day and can compensate more frequently.

To calculate the set and drift must keep track of your average speed and direction. you then plot your dead reckoning position along your track, you will have an approximate location of your position at all times.

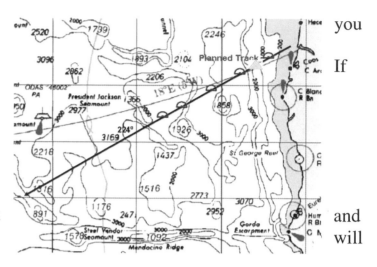

you If

When you obtain a position fix plot it on the same chart, it tell you where you really are

and will

located. Similar to the way a GPS calculates SOG and COG. Computing the true direction (COG) from the last position fix is simply the direction of the line between the two points.

On the first chart we see the vessel has a planned track of $224°$ and the last dead reckoning position we plotted was 100 miles down the track from the last position fix 20 hours earlier. The distance is based on a 5 knot speed and a course of $224°$.

When we plot our actual position from a position fix device, we see that in actuality we are south and ahead of track. Our COG was actually 211 $°$ and the

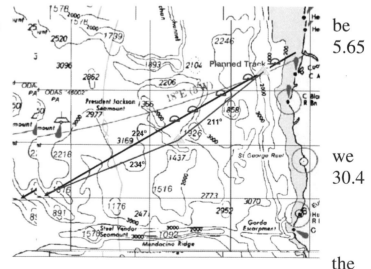

distance was 113 nautical miles. So the SOG would then be 113 nautical miles/20 hours or 5.65 knots.

If we plot the difference between the dead reckoning position and the fix position see that our set and drift are nm $154°$ for 20 hours or 30.4nm/20 hours =1.52nm/hour at $154°$. To remain on the planned track

we 30.4

the

set and drift must be compensated for by changing at least your course. If you must arrive at a specific time, the vessel's speed must also be modified.

To compensate for the set and drift we have several options. If for some <u>reason our vessel</u> must remain close to track, we could head on a reciprocal course to the 154° drift, 360- 154 = 206° and drive directly back to the planned track. This approach is not normally the best approach for traveling across the ocean and can be costly if you are driving a trawler burning fuel just to get back to the track.

If the actual track is not that important you could change course to compensate for the 1.52 nm force at 154° only and travel on a new track. This approach would require a bit of math to calculate the required course and speed and is well beyond the scope of this book, but worth learning if you get a chance. But if we look at the angle difference between where we thought we were headed and where we are actually going, we can simply say correcting the course to the right by 13° or 237° new course should get us close to the same direction of 224°.

Most cruisers would like to get back to their planned track since being too far off; they may miss the island of paradise they are heading for.

Using the same logic as before, since the 237° course calculated above will keep us heading on a 224° course when the earth's effects are thrown in, coming around more to the right will result in coming closer to the track. It then becomes up to you how quickly you desire to get back on track. The chart shows we desire to get back to the track at a certain point. Don't forget to add in the 13° to compensate for the southerly push so instead of steering 234° you need to head around 247° to get back near the point shown.

Changing course, speed and position will ultimately provide a new set of earth's factors that will invariably shift your SOG and COG in a new way. The more frequently you get position fixes, the closer you will probably stay to your planned track.

Track Error

Since we just looked at the fact that the earth's effects can result in your vessel not being where you think it is, it is important to pay attention. Look at your charts to see what obstructions might be around you. Pay attention to which way the wind is blowing even if you are not sailing. Find out what the predominate ocean currents are for the area you are transiting. From the basic information you obtain, you will have some idea what would happen if you were just sitting out there with the motor off and the sails down. Where would the vessel go? Chances are it will not just sit at the same Latitude and Longitude.

After you have determined where the boat will go with the earth's effects, establish a new track that incorporates the worse case scenario for position error as you travel on your planned track.

Are there obstructions within that area? Are you heading toward a shipping lane? Should you expect a lot of fishing vessels? Etc.

At the end of the day maybe, just maybe, you will have GPS for the entire trip and all the planning you did will not be needed. The other option, no planning because you have GPS, can be deadly.

Chapter 11 – Communications

VHF Radio use

Marine Very High Frequency (VHF) radio is powerful tool on board a vessel. To promote the use of VHF radios on boats, the FCC does not require a license for operation of VHF radios within the US waters by recreational vessels less than 20 meters long and not for hire. However, if you are planning trips, even to Canada, operate for hire or have a vessel longer than 20 meters, you should obtain an operator's permit and license. **Regardless of your license status, you are expected to follow and are responsible for all FCC regulations.**

Every boat on the water should have at least a portable VHF transceiver on board. The VHF radio is the key communications method on the water. In spite of this, many folks try to use their cell phones instead of VHF. VHF radio communications assure direct contact with other vessels around you. This is the best potential for safe boating. If you have an emergency and call out on channel 16, someone will answer.

Among the many channels available on the VHF transceiver, the key channels you should be aware of would include:

Channel	Use
16	Distress, Safety, and calling channel. The Coast Guard monitors this channel for emergencies. You may call for a friend, but should change to another channel as quickly as possible in order to keep the channel clear for emergencies and safety notifications by the Coast Guard.
22A	Coast Guard Liaison channel. Primarily used for conversations with the Coast Guard when they have been contacted on channel 16. The Coast Guard also broadcasts safety type messages on 22A, after announcing on channel 16 that they will be provided. The "A" means that this is channel 22 in the US. If your transceiver is selected to international, it will not pick up the Coast Guard on this channel.

24,25,26,27, 28, 84, 85, 86, and 87 are available for marine operators so you can make a phone call via your VHF radio. This service is not available in all areas, but the channels are not for general use.

13   Commercial ship communications to other ships to aid in navigation as well as communications with bridges and locks. If traveling with commercial traffic, it is a good channel to monitor so you know what the big guys are doing.

7A, 8, 10, 11, 18A, 19A, 21A, 23A, 67, 77, 79A, 80A, 81A, 82A, 83A, and 88A   Are not to be used by pleasure boats, commercial and or Government use only.

70   Digital Selective calling for radios equipped with this feature.

9, 68, 69, 71 Commercial and public use for general communications.

72   Commercial and public use only for ship to ship general communications.

Copy of above information contained on the CD for ease of printing: "VHF Channel Use Chart.doc" or at: http://wireless.fcc.gov/marine/vhfchanl.html

Based on the above chart you can call others on channel 16 and then shift to 9, 68, 69, 71, or if ship to ship communications you can also shift to 72 for communications. If you would like to contact a commercial ship to aid in the navigation and safe passage, channel 13 is a good place to go and monitor.

In some regions there maybe local networks on channel 5 that control shipping movements within the region, kind of like traffic control for airplanes.

The Coast Guard usually makes announcements on channel 22.

Most radios have a scan mode where they check several channels and if someone is talking, they stop and listen. I usually scan 16, 22, 13, and sometimes 5. If I feel snoopy, I might also scan 68 to see what folks are talking about up there on the common gab channel.

Communicating

If you happen to get in trouble while out on the water and it is life threatening, you can contact the Coast Guard on channel 16 and at the same time clear the channel of other traffic by calling "Mayday, Mayday, Mayday" followed by your call sign if applicable, and the name of your vessel. This should be repeated three times.

Example: Mayday, Mayday, Mayday, this is WB3792, Sailing vessel Green Ship - Mayday, Mayday, Mayday, this is WB3792, Sailing vessel Green Ship - Mayday, Mayday, Mayday, this is WB3792, Sailing vessel Green Ship, Over.

Upon being contacted back by the Coast Guard, you should be prepared to provide your latitude and longitude, nature of distress, number of people on board, status of wearing life jackets (Since it is a life threatening emergency the message should be "all persons on board have life jackets on."), seaworthiness of vessel, description of your vessel, and any other information requested by the Coast Guard.

If you are reporting another vessel in distress use "Mayday Relay" instead of "Mayday". Similar information will be requested by the Coast Guard about you and to the best of your ability the vessel in distress.

Mayday Relay, Mayday Relay, Mayday Relay, WB3792, Sailing vessel Green Ship - Mayday Relay, Mayday Relay, Mayday Relay, WB3792, Sailing vessel Green Ship - Mayday Relay, Mayday Relay, Mayday Relay, WB3792, Sailing vessel Green Ship, Over

For other vessel hearing the Mayday call, if there is no response to a Mayday call from the Coast Guard (you are a long way off shore), you should take action and respond to the call. Your response should be: the call sign and name of the vessel giving the Mayday call and then "Received Mayday". That should be followed with "This is (your call sign) and (vessel name)." Listen for others, but be prepared to aid the vessel in distress.

Example: WB3792, Sailing vessel Green Ship, Received Mayday, this is vessel WA5499, Avenger, over.

Remember the Coast Guard is not a towing service. In fact if all you need is a tow, they will try to get someone to help via VHF radio only. Should no one be willing to respond and assist you, they will call a towing service at your expense.

The next level of priority communications is "Pan". Similar to the Mayday communications, you should not try to hail other vessels when you hear "Pan Pan, Pan Pan, Pan Pan". It is used when safety of personnel is in danger, but not immediate. For example, you are adrift because your vessel is out of gas or the engine will just not start.

The next level of communications on channel 16 is the safety signal: "Security" pronounced "Securita, Securita, Securita". The Coast guard will often identify notification of storm warnings and other messages that may affect the ability of vessels to maintain safe marine navigation.

As a side note you will also be issued a Maritime Mobile Service Identification Number (MMSI) that may be used to identify your vessel when you purchase a radio that has digital selective calling (DSC) capability. DSC is available on most modern radios for both VHF and HF radio. In an emergency, you can send a digital signal that includes your latitude, longitude, and your ships station identification number (MMSI).

It is important that you obtain an MMSI because the U.S. Coast Guard (plans to) uses this information to help speed search and rescue operations if you should get into trouble at sea.

If you are not planning to obtain an FCC license (VHF use only within US waters) you may obtain an MMSI by contacting either BoatUS, Sea Tow Service International, Inc., or MariTEL.

DSC may also be used between boaters to call instead of hailing on channel 16. If you program your radio to include other boats MMSI number, the radio can send a digital signal to one or more radios that actually changes the channel number of all radios to a designated channel and sits waiting for the two or more people to commence their conversation. This is not a private channel, but simply a digital way of calling/hailing other boaters.

Single Side Band – HF Radio

Single side band (SSB) communications operates in the high frequency (HF) range and can allow you to talk around the world if conditions are right. HF radio can be used to make telephone calls, obtain weather fax reports, send and receive e-mail, talk to other ships and or shore stations, and even call in emergencies when you are too far off shore for VHF marine radio communications. SSB is a good thing to have on board if you plan to go off shore.

If you have one on board the following are some tips on how to best use it. If not and you do not have an electronics background, you might want to talk to your local Marine Electronics store.

Operation of HF radio does require an FCC restricted radiotelephone operator's permit and station license. The good news is that if you obtain the station license you are good to go for VHF, Radar and HF radio all in one license. The license does cost a few dollars, but is a lot less that the fine for using your equipment and not having a license. The license is presently good for 10 years. My operator permit has no expiration date. However, things change so check with the FCC to be sure.

Some good reading on the subject of licenses:
http://wireless.fcc.gov/marine/fctsht14.html

Use of the VHF and HF radios is mostly just common sense. Hopefully common sense is something you have already attained or radio operation will be the least of your worries on a boat at sea.

Basic courtesy includes listening for others talking before transmitting and not transmitting on channels not assigned to you.

So be polite when you operate any radio transmitter. HF radio should not be considered a CB radio, good buddy. HF Radio is a professional tool. Improper use can pack a $10,000 fine or even jail time for serious violations.

HF radios may be used by dialing in the actual frequency you want to use or by dialing in the ITU channel number. The channel numbers are easy to dial in and do not contain a decimal number. Frequency- 2,182.0 would dial in "21820 enter" and ITU channel 424 would be selected by entering "424 enter".

An overview on ITU channels available can be found at:
http://www.naval.com/hf-freq.htm

http://www.navcen.uscg.gov/marcomms/high_frequency/rtchansi.htm

http://www.navcen.uscg.gov/marcomms/high_frequency/rtchan.txt

Antennas

Most sail boats utilize the center section of the back stay as an antenna for HF equipment. If your planned boat has HF and it is using the back stay as the antenna, the backstay will have insulators near the top and bottom of the stay. There should also be a wire connected to the wire in between the insulators that probably goes back into your boat someplace. That connecting wire normally goes to an antenna tuning box to make the antenna the right size for all the frequencies the radio transmits on. The antenna tuning box adds and subtracts coils and capacitors to compensate for the length of the fixed back stay antenna at various frequencies. To transmit with maximum power out, the antenna must be at least ¼ wavelength long and have a good ground plane to reflect another ¼ wavelength. You could also use a ½ wave antenna. That means the antenna would need to be twice as long. Wavelength in meters = 300/the frequency in MHz

Example ¼ wavelength antenna 4,000 KHz, or 4Mz would be ¼ of 300/4MHz or 18.75 meters (about 60 feet) while a ½ wavelength antenna would be 37.5 meters. Little to big for my mast! At 23,000 KHz or 23 MHz the ¼ wavelength would only be approximately 3.3 Meters or 6.5 meters for ½ wavelength antennas. The antenna tuning box causes the fixed length antenna you have to look like all of these lengths as you tune up through the bands. Connecting your radio directly to the wire would probably result in blowing up the radio output transistors, so don't go there.

Since the ¼ wave antenna requires a reflected wave in the ground plane it is important to have a good ground plane. If you have a steal or aluminum boat you are good to go, but those of us with plastic boats need to make sure everything is connected up. Originally Sunnyside had copper strips connecting all the metal parts. It appears as though a lot of it had been replaced by heavy gauge wire. I found a link that had corroded though when trouble shooting weak reception of signal on WWV (National time standard on 5,000, 10,000 and 15,000 KHz). When repairing the corroded links all of a sudden I had strong signals. This sure made me a believer in ground plane.

There are also devices you can purchase to make a great connection to the sea that are mounted on the outside of the boat's hull. "Dynaplates" are suppose to be very good at providing a great ground plane.

It is possible to use whip antennas in stead of the back stay long wire. Some can be used without the antenna coupler and some still require the coupler. So if that is what you would like to use on your boat, check with a marine electronics vender.

If you are using your mast's back stay as the antenna, don't forget that when you need it most might be when you lose your mast. You can rig a temporary antenna that will work fairly well by stringing a piece of #10 wire approximately the same length as the one on your mast along your boat. What ever is the tallest structure remaining on your boat is a good place to start. Some form of insulation at both ends is still important. Emergency antennas are also available for sale, but given they are basically just a piece of wire and a couple of insulators, they seem a bit pricey. They do look nice though.

HF Emergency communication channels

Like VHF radio there are hailing and emergency channels. Radio manufactures are required to have HF radios start up in the primary hailing and emergency channel 2,182.0 KHz. Other emergency channels include 4,125.0 KHz, 6,215.0 KHz, 8,291.0 KHz, 12,290.0 KHz, 16, 420.0 KHz, and ITU channel 606.

US Coast Guard calling is done on ITU channel 424, 601, and 1624.

Weather FAX

NOAA has broadcast stations on the Pacific and Atlantic coasts and broadcasts weather fax information at various times during the day and night.

On the left hand coast, Pacific, we get FAX transmission out of California on the following frequencies: 4346, 8682, 1286, and 22527

In order to receive the FAX information you must detune the receiver by 1.9 KHz to get to the lower sideband or in other words tune the HF receiver to: 4344.1, 8680.1, 1284.1, or 22525.1 KHz to pick up the FAX signal.

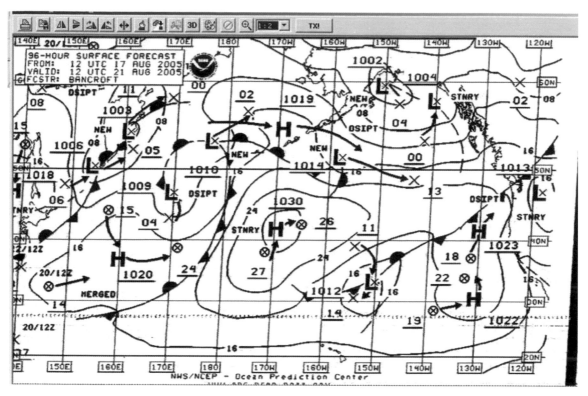

There are many software programs that run on your PC that will create a FAX display from the signal displaying a weather forecast. I have been using "JVCOM32" I purchased over the internet.
http://www.jvcomm.de/indexe.html   JVCOM32 has worked out great for me and the cost was minimal. There is also a free trial version available.

There is also a ham free ware called wxsat that works well also.
http://www.hffax.de/html/hauptteil_wxsat.htm

The above example "96-HOUR SURFACE FORECAST" was a screen display from a NOAA weather FAX recorded at sea on a trip we made down the Pacific coast in 2005.

Knowing the weather forecast is a must when you are out in the ocean in a boat. If you look closely, you can see the outline of the west coast. With a good HF system you can get excellent forecasts from weather broadcasts around the world for those locations.

Telephone Calls via HF Radio

A high seas operator can be reached on WLO radio on the east coast and KLB radio on the west coast. Actually it is possible to use either channel on either coast if the conditions are right since HF radio can go around the world. WLO radio owns both stations. They can be reached at 334.666.5110 or via the internet at www.wloradio.com to set up service.

When making a call you first contact WLO/KLB radio on channels (WLO) 1212, 1641, 0r 2237 – (KLB) 417, 805, 1209, or 1624. A typical call would progress as follows:

WLO, WLO, WLO this is the sailing vessel Sunnyside (vessel name) WDA 1234 (call sign) operating on channel 2-2-3-7. Over.
Pause and listen.

WLO, WLO, WLO this is the sailing vessel Sunnyside (vessel name) WDA 5497 (call sign) operating on channel 2-2-3-7. Over.

Pause and listen.

WLO, WLO, WLO this is the sailing vessel Sunnyside operating on channel 2-2-3-7 over.

When the operator answers he or she will ask you what service he or she can provide. I have a credit card on file with the service so when I make a call it knows how to get paid. You can also give credit card information over the air (if you have the guts), call collect, etc. The phone call is a bit pricey, but compared to stringing wire after your boat it is quite reasonable at $4-5 per minute. Be sure and keep the teenagers away from the WLO/KLB radio telephone calls.

If by chance that the WLO or KLB operator does not answer your call, be sure and be courteous and say something like, "Negative contact, Sunnyside, WDA 1234 clear".

When you have reached your party on the call, remember to say "over" before releasing the microphone key to tell your party it is OK for him or her to talk now. You cannot hear someone while the mike key is depressed.

When your telephone party has hung up, be sure and standby for the operator to call you back. He or she will ask if you have completed your call and if you would like to make another. Your replay should be something like "WLO, this is the sailing vessel Sunnyside. We are done. Thank you." WLO radio will sign off and then you should say something like "Sunnyside WDA 1234 clear."

You will have to monitor a WLO/KLB radio channel if you want to be available for people to call you. People can call WLO/KLB radio or just dial "O" and ask for the high seas operator and they can try to reach you at sea.

Ham Radio Use

If you are a licensed Amateur Radio Operator (Ham), you can also use the Ham frequencies on your ham radio. You may listen to Ham frequencies without a license, but it is illegal to transmit on those channels, except in an emergency case. Most HF radios may be or are set up to communicate on both Ham bands as well as the Marine bands. I recently took three tests and qualified for the Amateur Extra license. (*AD7XL*)

Ham radio does have some real advantages <u>for e-mails</u> and voice calls for free, so check it out. I highly recommend a General Class License for all cruisers. Weather, phone patches, email, and general help are the Ham plusses.

On a trip to La Paz Mexico, my wife broke her ankle. While she was traveling in an ambulance to La Paz, we continued on the boat to La Paz. We were able to get phone patches and keep track of their progress, for free as a Ham.

E-mail at Sea

E-mail at sea is a real cool option. You can utilize your single sideband High Frequency radio to receive and send e-mail. However, the new generation of sailors seem to be shifting to satellite e-mail and communications for coastal operation as a result of the Globalstar reasonable rate structure and high reliability. If you are going offshore, the cost goes up and the data rates go down.

HF E-mail

To send and receive e-mail from your SSB HF transceiver you must connect your computer to a special purpose modem. The "Proctor" compatible modems are a bit pricey, but have set the standard for HF communications. This modem will translate incoming tones and create outgoing tones to send your thoughts to someone you left back home.

Modern day SSB receivers frequently have the modem connections built in, but you can purchase a modem and connect it to an older transceiver.

A subscription to a service such as Sailmail, or if you are a Ham you may use Winlink for free, will allow you to send and receive email on SSB HF radio.

Satellite Communications

Satellite communications are about where cell phone providers were ten years ago. It took that long for them to figure out that if the equipment is there, more calls do not increase the cost, so more customers at lower, bulk style plans will help keep things alive.

There a are several providers of Satellite communications. We already discussed Globalstar. Globalstar covers the land and coastal areas around the world.

Iridium provides complete worldwide coverage. Data rates are slower than Globalstar.

There have been many service providers that will set you up with equipment and service similar to the cell phone operators.

You can even rent Satellite phones for as little at $19.95 per week. For example, from the internet at the time of publishing this book, the following satellite packages were available.

Globalstar advertisement	Iridium advertisement
1. As low as $19.95 per week! 2. Superb Voice Quality and Reliability! 3. Convenient U.S. satellite number 4. Lowest Per Minute Cost $0.95 5. 9600 bps internet access 6. 3.75 hours of talk time http://www.globalstar.com/	1. As low as $19.95 per Week! 2. Truly global satellite phone! 3. No long distance or roaming charges! 4. Voice, Paging, SMS, Emergency 911. 5. Two-Way Global Voice & Data. 6. All ocean areas, air routes & all landmasses - even the Poles.

Making Telephone Calls Home

How do you make international calls to the family at home when you are out there cruising? That was a question my wife Pat had for some time and she did not like the $1.50+/minute answers.

There are a lot of ways to communicate: Cell Phone; Sat Phone; HF Radio Marine Operators; Calling Cards; Money at a pay phone (if you can find one) just to name a few we thought of immediately. They all have the same thing in common; they cost a lot per minute when you are outside the United States. (Could be close to $2.00/minute with a monthly or annual charge in most cases) Even cell calls from Victoria Canada across the water to Friday Harbor can be cost prohibitive.

Two US cell providers now have agreements in place throughout Mexico allowing you to use a US cell phone in Mexico at a reasonable cost. So call your service provider and get signed up if you are headed to Mexico.

One method that did not jump out at us was using the internet to do calls. Purchasing a $25-30 headset with a microphone built in and then down-load the free software and get connected to a service like "Skype" will significantly reduce your call home cost.

There are other services available, but we liked Skype as Skype provided a free software package, the software is easy to use, and the computer to computer phone calls are free. You also pay very little for the actual calls to land lines as well. Actually they have a service for less than $30 that adds voice mail and free calls for the year if you do not want to set up calls to your family member's computers.

Another similar service, Magic Jack provides international calling via the internet for about $20 per year.

Most ports have internet these days and even if it costs you for that service it can be much cheaper than a traditional phone. Many places charge around $1.75 for an hour's use of pay internet. That is slightly higher than the cost of a minute HF Marine, Cell, or Sat Phone. For that hour, you can call everyone you know and still get the latest weather information in the background.

We have found that most Baja California Marinas provide internet at no cost.

Final note on communications:

- Plan to have a communications device for long distance communications.
  - If SSB HF radio is your choice, get at least a general class Ham License and a Practor modem for email
  - If Sat Phone is your direction, make sure you have phone numbers and a method to connect to you computer for email.
- If headed for Mexico, get your cell phone set up on a Mexico plan.

Chapter 12 – The Horizon

The distance to the horizon is a very valuable thing to understand when boating as well as what is effected by that distance.

Since the earth is round, our line of sight basically goes off the edge of the earth similar to what people believed ships did before Columbus sailed the Ocean Blue.

Similarly high frequency signals do the same as the light waves we see through our vision. When they pass the horizon they go out into space.

VHF Radio is Very High Frequency and is good for a distance approximately the distance to the horizon.

Line of sight is also true for radar signals. When you are looking on the 25 mile range on your radar, you are looking for weather coming in only as most radar mounted on sail boats do not report vessels more than about 10 miles depending on the height of the vessel.

If we stand higher we can see farther and likewise if tall things are in the distance, we can see them farther away. So line of sight is based on height of both what you are looking at and where you are looking from. Taller is better! This applies to both your VHF radio and your radar.

The horizon is approximately only 5 miles when you are 17 feet above sea level. At 30 feet in the air we can only see 6.71 miles. So basically VHF radio, AIS, and Radar have a range on the water to another vessel of less than 10 miles. Communicating to a shore station might be a lot farther as they might be sitting on a very high tower. In saying all of this, sometimes things happen and it is possible for even VHF to skip, but not very often.

HF radio actually uses reflected waves off the ionosphere and bounces back and forth to the earth allowing very long range communications with many gaps in communications between bounces.

For more information on communications, check out the communications training on my web site. http://sunnyside-adventure.webs.com/trainingforsailors.htm

Chapter 13 – Radar

Getting good at running your radar unit can be more important than knowing how to sail when the fog is so thick that you cannot see your bow light. The time to practice is when you can see what is out there. Radar may be used for both vessel avoidance and when within sight of land, it may also provide fix positions.

The basics

Most people are aware that Radar was developed just before World War II. It was being tested on December 7, 1941 when the Japanese bombed Pearl Harbor. The radar operators actually saw the Japanese airplanes arriving, but no one had any faith in the system at the time and assumed the received signals were either US planes returning or just bad signals.

Radar has progressed a lot since WWII. What was once too expensive for anyone to use but the military, is now common place for the average cruising vessel.

Radar transmits a very directional signal, then waits in the receive mode until it hears echoes from that transmitted signal. The display starts drawing a picture from the center of the display to the outer edge of the display as it waits for returned echoes. The time it takes for the trace to move from the center of the display to the outer edge of the display is the same time that it will take the transmitted signal to move from the antenna to a location the same distance as the scale you are on times 2. In other words, if you are on the five mile scale, the transmitted signal will go out to 5 miles, hit a target and return to the antenna. The display trace will be at the maximum for the scale when the return signal arrives and will create a mark proportional to the amount of energy that was received at the maximum range point.

The transmitted signal does not stop when it gets to the scale's maximum range but continues on. The transmitter, however, stops listening for the return signal and goes back to the transmit mode for another transmit pulse. The size of the returned signal is proportional to the size or actually the ability of the target to reflect the signal. Metal boats reflect more than plastic or wood boats. So don't forget to install that radar reflector on your boat, unless it is steel, so you can be seen by other radars.

The pulse that is transmitted travels at the speed of light and as you may have figured out already the display goes from the center to the maximum at ½ the speed of light.

Another factor that has to be considered is the radar is displaying a relative direction of targets. That means that contacts displayed at 000 degrees on your radar are coming from beyond the bow of your boat. The radar's right side (090), left (270), and the bottom of the display (180), then represents the contacts coming from the Starboard, Port, and Aft of your vessel respectively. Some radar installations may also have a heading reference provided so that the top of the screen may be selected as true north. The advantage of this is primarily that as your vessel changes heading, the contacts are always displayed in the same location on the Radar display. The down side is, unless you are heading north you could be headed directly for a target and not know it when sailing without a dedicated radar operator. I prefer relative bearings as you have plenty to think about contact positions. If I see a vessel that will be in front of me on the radar, I know I have to do something.

Using your Radar

After many hours operating radar on a submarine, I did not feel it necessary to purchase a book or take a course on radar operation. If you have not operated radar before, I would suggest you do so as the following information is only the basics. The skill required to obtain radar contact solutions in a timely manor is as important as learning to sail.

When another vessel is a long distance away it is difficult to tell if it is going to run over you or pass a mile away. It is important that you determine the closest point of approach (CPA) for each vessel you are tracking in the fog or even in the daytime.

Since radar typically provides a relative speed and direction of contact vessels, you can rough out a vector right on the radar screen to determine when another vessel will be at its closest point to your vessel or more appropriately the CPA.

While in the Navy we used a grease pencil on the display. With my radar I use the cursor to mark one spot then the contact for another. Works well.

The examples below use larger ranges than typically seen on boat radars. The Radar horizon for most boats is less than 8 nautical miles. Actual range for your boat will be dependent on antenna height above the water and the target height.

The Quick CPA Check

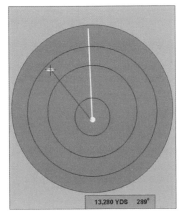

1. When we obtain a trace of another ship, run your cursor out to the location of that ship as a marker. In the Navy we used grease pencils, but what a mess. Note the cursor bearing and range digital readout indicate the contact is at 13,280 Yards at relative bearing 289°. Keeping in mind that 2000 Yards is approximately one nautical mile, the contact is a bit over 6 ½ miles away. Note the range rings

are at 5,000 yards per ring and the maximum range should then be 15,000 yards or 7.5 Nautical Miles. It is important that you get a feel for the numbers whenever you look at the screen. There is no need to panic right now, for the contact is a long way off.

2. Exactly five minutes later we check our contact again and find out she is getting closer and headed in front of us. Do we panic now? Not yet! Let's run a line from our cursor through the contact past our vessel.

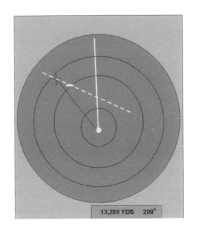

3. According to our line the contact coming towards us will pass over 6,000 yards in front of us if neither of us changes speed or course. Quickly, how far? 6000 yards is over three nautical miles away. If the visibility is not good, we might not even see the other ship.

4. It is important though to keep verifying the track the other ship is on and to maintain the course we are on. If in five minutes we check where the contact is and we find that it is now at about 7500 yards and close to the CPA (Closest Point of Approach). Keep a close watch till the contact has passed CPA.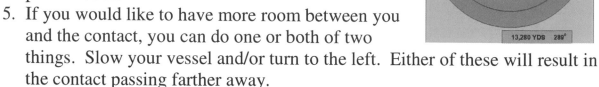

5. If you would like to have more room between you and the contact, you can do one or both of two things. Slow your vessel and/or turn to the left. Either of these will result in the contact passing farther away.

6. It is important to remember that the speed and coarse you are tracking is really a combination of your speed and the other vessel's <u>speed. If you</u> were to turn right it will take longer for the other vessel to pass by and therefore he would be closer to your vessel.

7. The term zero bearing rate is used when the contact is walking down the cursor line. If there is no bearing change that means that you and the other contact will meet at some point and the out come will not be pretty. For a zero bearing rate contact, you can turn right, turn left, speed up, or slow down and the bearing rate will change to a more or less favorable one. It is important to remember that the contact and you are creating the zero bearing rate, not just the other boat. The recommended coarse correction would be just like when you are driving your car, turn to the right 10-15 degrees and then re-check the new CPA. Typically it is understood that you will strive for a Port to Port passing unless you have an agreement with the other vessel to do otherwise.

8. Along the lines of an agreement, it is always a good idea to try and communicate with the other vessel(s) you see on your radar, especially during reduced visibility.

CPA Example two:

If you have Maneuvering board paper, you can plot your contact on the paper. This is a more accurate method, but more time consuming as well. I like to use the display method above, but it may improve your understanding of the concept of CPA by going through a Maneuvering board solution once.

Note: This example uses very large distance measurements as an example. Our radars do not see vessels 70 miles away, but it makes the math easy to show the larger numbers as an example.

We have plotted three points:
1. 1000 – 70 miles @ bearing 315°
2. 1030 – 56 miles @ bearing 318°
3. 1100 – 40 miles @ bearing 326°

The red line shows the distance covered in one hour. (Approximately 3.0 nautical miles or 30 NM/hour)

To determine when the CPA will occur, measure the distance to the perpendicular line to the center point. It is approximately 35 miles as shown by the green line. Using ratios we can quickly determine the time of the CPA and we can read the distance to be 17 NM.

So:

$$\frac{30NM}{60 \text{ min}} = \frac{35 \text{ NM}}{X} \qquad OR \qquad \frac{35 * 60}{30} = 70 \text{ Minutes to CPA}$$

The plots are included on a paper chart called a Maneuvering board on the next page. Paper maneuvering boards work well and the contact's true speed and course may also be determined on the Maneuvering Board. However, to avoid contacts, the appropriate action may be taken with relative information only. It may be very difficult to sail, watch the radar and run a Maneuvering Board while single handing.

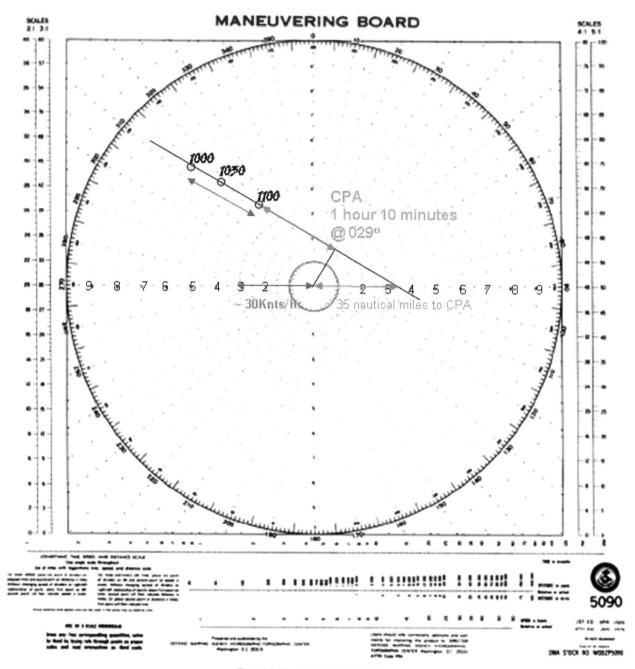

Figure 3.16 - Maneuvering Board.

Other Calculations to give you a feel for the situation at hand

1. Another quick calculation you can do from the radar scope is a rough relative speed. We know the relative direction and if we look at the distance covered in the five minutes it was about 4000 Yards. So 4000/5 is the speed per minute or 800 Yards per minute. Then we could calculate the speed by multiplying by 60 (minutes in an hour) and dividing by 2000 (yards in a nautical mile).

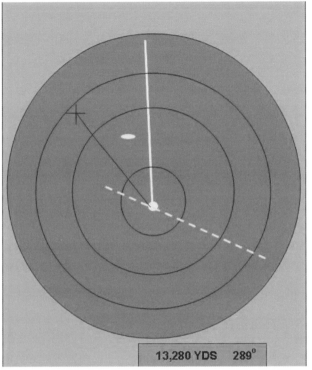

13,280 YDS   289°

Since:

$$60/2000 = 0.03$$

So a quick calculation is:

Yards/Minute X 0.03

Or

$$800X\ 0.03 = 24\ \text{nm/hour}$$

2. We could also walk the relative bearing line back to the center of the radar scope and see that the relative course is approximately 125°.

True Contact Speed and direction

3. From relative course and speed, and knowing your course and speed, you can plot those vectors on a maneuvering board plot. Then you can determine what the resultant vector is, which would be the contact's true course and speed.

An example of a vector solution for the other ship's true course and speed calculations are shown in the adjacent figure.

Steps:

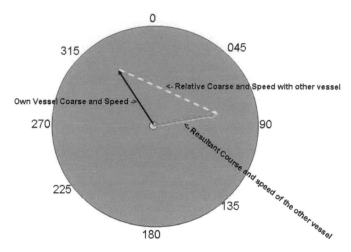

1. Plot the relative movement of the other vessel on a maneuvering board with times of plotted range and bearing.
2. Plot own vessel's course and true speed. For example, our vessel is headed at 320 degrees and 20 knots.
3. Determine the relative speed of the other vessel.
4. Plot the relative speed from the end of your own vessel's vector at the same angle as the relative movement of the other vessel.
5. Draw a new vector from the center to the end of the relative course and speed vector.
6. The new vector is the actual speed and direction vector of the other vessel.

The course and speed shown are not scaled to the above radar examples, but just a relative indication of the steps needed to determine the other ship's true course and speed. To ease the calculation of true coarse and speed, be sure and pick up some maneuvering board sheets.

If we now use the maneuvering board we can get a more accurate calculation of the other vessel's speed and direction. (See maneuvering board next page.)

1. Using the same contact information as the last Maneuvering board problem, we know the contact is traveling at a relative 30 NM/Hr. Let's assume our vessel is headed 330° at 20 NM/Hr. Plot that vector (Red) on the Maneuvering board.
2. Then move the relative direction vector down to the end point of your own vessel's vector. (Dashed line)
3. Draw a new line to the end of the other vessel's relative movement vector. (Blue Vector)
4. The new line is the true speed and course of the other vessel. [18 NM/Hr @ 088°]

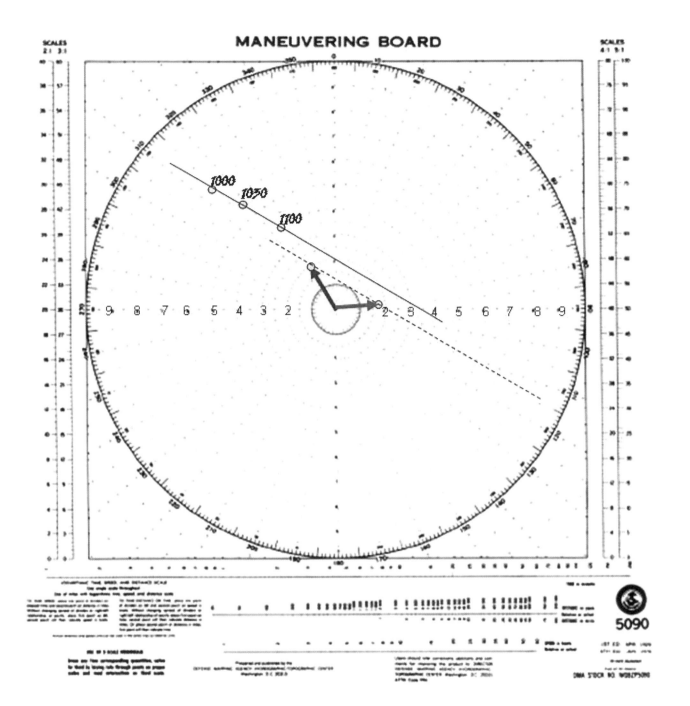

For simplification we have used round numbers for demonstration purposes.

Things used to make the Maneuvering board fit the problem:

1. Scale things – The chart is scaled 2-1, 3-1, 4-1, and 5-1. You could use a factor of 0.5 to make things larger. For example, $2 = 1$, $3 = 1.5$, $4 = 2$, etc.
2. It is not necessary to have an hour's worth of information to calculate CPA or true speed. You can scale your numbers by the same method as utilized before.

$$\frac{\text{Distance of Relative Movement} * 60 \text{ (min.)}}{\text{Period of Movement (min.)}} = \text{Nautical Miles per hour}$$

Chapter 14 – CARD

The Collision Avoidance Radar Detector (CARD) is a very good low cost item to have on your boat. When you are not using your radar, the CARD can listen for other vessels traveling along that are using their radar.

Basically it is four (4) little radar receivers in a rail mountable container that looks like a large GPS antenna. The receivers are located 90 degrees apart so that you can get an approximate direction of the radar that is coming at you.

Each receiver drives a small display in the cockpit to identify to the helmsperson a general idea where the radar signal is coming from. It tells you where to look.

CARD is a low power consumption device as it only draws about 0.045 amps from a 12 volt battery source.

I believe that the CARD system may be purchased only via the internet at:
http://www.survivalsafety.com/

In December 2010, the approximate cost of CARD was: $ 500.00 USD

I have had mine on board for ten years now with no issues and it has been very helpful to keep me out of trouble.

Chapter 15 – GPS

Global Position Satellites (GPS) has been one of the greatest developments in navigation since the Sextant. The basics of how a GPS position fix is calculated may not be all that important to a cruising sailor. However, understanding how a GPS works solidifies the other methods of obtaining a position fix as basically they are the same concepts.

My last active duty assignment was actually at a Navy station in Minnesota where we injected signals into the earlier version of the satellites. The earlier version worked on a combination of time and Doppler frequency shift.
The Doppler position satellites worked on the same basis of the sound effect of a train coming toward you. The frequency of the oncoming train sounds higher as it approaches, and then gets lower when the train is headed away from you. The point, at which the train's sound becomes equal to the sound the train is actually putting out, is when it is at your position.

In a boat with a satellite that orbits from the North Pole to the South Pole, the point the received frequency is equal to that the satellite is transmitting is the point where the satellite's latitude equals your latitude. The longitude is calculated based on the shape of the curves of the frequency. The equipment to calculate all of this was expensive and complex. We only had a hand full of operational satellites in those days, so frequently there could be no positions calculated for hours at a time. I remember having to set up for a Navigation Satellite pass. We would track one for 20 minutes and hope to get one accurate position fix. How things change.

Today's civilian GPS computes your Latitude and Longitude similar to the older popular Loran 'C' except there is no master station. The GPS receiver locks on to multiple satellites and tracks them as long as they are in view. There are around 24 satellites now that are orbiting the sky so there are always satellites available. The satellites tell you which satellite they are, where they are at that time, and what time it is to make sure we are all using the right time. When we lock on to at least three satellites we can get a reasonably good position fix by measuring the time it takes the signal to get to our vessel. More satellites provide better position accuracy to some extent.

If we have a position fix and then calculate another fix, we can calculate our speed (SOG) and direction (COG) over ground based on the difference between the two fix positions and the elapsed time. How Cool is that!

One thing to remember though is that is the COG and SOG are not necessarily the speed through the water and the heading of your vessel. That is because the earth's effects have impacts on your movement. For example if we are out of gear and not making way on the engine or sails, but have a 15 knot wind blowing us sideways at 4 knots, the GPS will give us a COG of the direction of the beam and a SOG of 4 knots. If we get underway on the engine the new COG and SOG will be a combination of both the earth effects and our engine's driving the vessel forward. The GPS will in actuality calculate the vector sum of all the movement without using trigonometry. The GPS knows you were at some location and then another now.

The accuracy of your position fixes on a GPS will vary some. The basic GPS may get you within 12 feet. Shore based transmitters and geostationary satellites enhance the accuracy of the system as they provide correction to the marine GPS receiver. This more sophisticated GPS is called a Differential GPS (DGPS). Basically, a DGPS receives another shore based or satellite signal that has calculated the error from the satellite GPS signal. Since the stationary based transmitter already knows where it is located, the error in the difference in the position fix it sees must be system error. The stationary station then transmits a signal that the DGPS unit picks up and uses as a correction factors for the final calculated positions. DGPS may get you even within a meter or two.

The tricky part of GPS

Many boaters develop an undying trust for the GPS position. While the position fixes are usually very good, frequently the chart information it is plotted on may not be as accurate. Water tends to move the bottom around so depths may change and points may extend. Many of the charts were developed some time ago and the charts are not updated very often.

It is not uncommon in a small river to have your track on your chart plotter showing you on the shore. Some of the error is a function of the GPS position accuracy and a lot of the position error will be the electronic chart data on which you are plotting the GPS position. Unfortunately, plotting on paper charts would not be more accurate and would clearly be more time consuming. So don't forget about your depth finder as it tells you the current depth regardless of GPS or chart inaccuracies.

Keys to success with your GPS:

1. Use GPS units as a navigation tool only.
2. Utilize the other instruments on your vessel to make sure everything makes sense.
3. When in doubt don't be afraid to pull out the paper charts or get position fixes from other sources.
4. Remember the electronics and all the other tools on your boat to get from point A to point B are just that, tools.
5. The Captain of the vessel is the primary navigation tool to get from point A to point B. All other tools are only input tools to help the Captain make the best decisions possible.

Chapter 16 – AIS

In the recent past the US Coast Guard has established a new system called Automatic Identification System or AIS.

All commercial vessels have been mandated to transmit a digital VHF signal on two channels (159MHz and 162 MHz). The signals provide information on that vessel such as Name of vessel, MSI number, present Latitude, present Longitude, Course, Speed, Course over Ground (COG), Speed over Ground (SOG), Destination, Vessel Length, Vessel Beam, closest point of approach (CPA), Time of CPA, etc.

The best use of this data for a cruiser is clearly to have the data displayed on the chart plotter in the cockpit. An AIS compatible chart plotter will place a ship symbol at the location of the latitude and longitude last sent. The plotted vessel then moves along with the information as received by the AIS receiver. The details of what else may be available and how it is displayed to the operator is a function of the chart plotter, but in general the data sent by the commercial vessel should be available.

AIS receivers come in two types, single channel and dual channel. If I was in a fast moving power boat I would have purchased the dual channel, however the single channel unit will provide all the same information if you wait long enough. The single channel unit shifts back and forth between the two frequencies and will eventually collect all the ship data being transmitted by the commercial vessel.

In practice it appears as though the commercial vessels are providing a direct feed from the ships GPS for much of the data. I have experienced that some ships indicate it traveling at 15 knots at 180 degrees heading and the location is at anchor. So some of the data must be manually input, or they have a lot of chain out…. The implementation of Class B AIS for use by recreational vessels has made this worse. Many boaters leave their AIS transmitter on while in a marina resulting in alarms for others coming into a marina. If you get a transmitter, turn it off when not in use.

Depending on the chart plotter alarming for vessels that are within a distance window (getting to close) or will be to close to you in a time you specify. This feature alone makes the whole system worth the cost to implement.

Installing an AIS receiver is very simple. It requires an antenna, 12 volts DC, and outputs a NEMA signal on an RS 232 connector. The output is simply connected to the NEMA input on the chart plotter display.

The Antenna can range in cost from almost nothing to a $100. You can also purchase a splitter that will connect the receiver to your boats VHF antenna. In my case I calculated the ½ wave length of the 159 MHz to be about a meter and stripped a meter of shield off a piece of RG58 I had with a BNC connector already on it and mounted the stripped wire in my closet next to the navigation station that gives me about 4-5 mile range.

There are also standalone models that provide a separate display for the AIS detected vessels. Not Recommended. It is all about safety at sea.

Warning: Just because you have AIS does not mean you should depend on it finding other vessels for you. Safety at sea means the skipper is paying attention to all aspects of the trip. If the electronic modules are used to backup good seamanship, your vessel will have the highest probability of returning from voyages. That also includes GPS, Radar etc. They are tools to help not the safety net we would sometimes like them to be.

Chapter 17 – Loran 'C'

LOng RAnge Navigation or Loran 'C' (Loran) has been available for widespread use since the late 1970's. The predecessor, Loran 'A' was developed back during World War II, but was less accurate. A few years back, many folks, including the government, felt that it was a dinosaur compared to the accurate fixes provided by GPS and no longer needed for navigation. After the terrorist attacks on the US, 9/11/2001, there were several situations where the government was considering turning off GPS so that GPS would not be available for the enemies of the US. At some point the US government decided Loran was a viable navigation method and instead of de-commissioning the stations, the transmitters were upgraded and the power for the stations is being significantly increased.

Loran is a very simple form of navigation which uses at least three shore based transmitters to define latitude and longitude (a FIX). Each network of Loran stations has at least one master station and typically two or more slave stations. Simply stated the master station transmits first and has a code on its signal that indicates it is the master. The slave stations cannot transmit their message until specified times later. Loran 'C' broadcasts on 100,000 Hz.

The Loran receiver detects the master and knows that a certain delay will occur before the slave signals start coming in. The cool part is that it takes additional time for the signals to get to you, even at the speed of light, based on how far from the master and slave stations your boat is located. Kind of like the radar ranging FIX, the Loran receiver measures your time delays from master and slaves and then calculates a FIX where the time delays cross.

The modern receivers are usually simple to operate and continuously display your Latitude and Longitude. The key to good positions is to reset the loran occasionally to what your GPS says the position is at the time. From there the Loran will keep good track of your position and provide continuous FIXes. The error in position is as a result of the speed of radio signals over land and sea being different. "Overland Phase Corrections" may be inserted into the Loran receiver to compensate for the error in position.

Similar to the GPS the Loran can provide other information such as speed made good, course, Velocity to destination, time to destination. You can also enter waypoints in the Loran and follow those points similar to a GPS.

Typical alarms include Cross-Track Error alarms, Boarder alarms, Arrival alarms, and Anchor Watch alarm. Sound familiar? When GPS became popular it had to provide all the information that Loran was already providing in order to make it a viable product.

Since Loran is a shore based navigation system, it has a limited capability for use. The original transmitters provided positions out to about 1200 miles. It is possible that with the higher power transmitters installed in the early 2000's it may extend the usable area for Loran receivers. The key would be the ability to discern the location of the master and slave units with adequate signal. As you move farther away from the shore location, the difference of the station locations becomes very small relative to the distance you are located from the stations.

With the upgrades of the Loran system, manufactures are developing combined GPS/Loran receivers. Combining the two systems, GPS and Loran, will have new accuracy and features. One new feature is supposed to be own ship's heading read out, even sitting at the dock in addition to COG. Adding ship's heading to the already great accuracy provided by GPS will significantly enhance the navigation capabilities of the average sailor.

Note added November 2010: The US LORAN system was turned off in 2010. There is a proposed project that has not been funded by the US Government to replace the system with an enhanced version that would be more accurate, provide time, and other digital information. We can only hope LORAN will return someday to give us a backup method of navigation.

Chapter 18 – Weather

Why Learn about Weather

Frequently sailors, mountain climbers, and even hikers hit the trail without consideration of the weather and soon find themselves in trouble. You may have heard some of the many reports each year telling about narrow escapes, injuries and in too many cases, loss of life.

A couple of years ago, a couple left from the West Coast in a 52 foot boat headed for Hawaii in December. When the boat was dismasted, and they were towed in by the Coast Guard, the skipper said: "I thought it might be a bit late in the season to get started, but we just ran late". This one was a very poor judgment call as even a quick look at the pilot charts for the north Pacific would have given him a clue that it was not going to be a fun trip.

Most cruising skippers take along friends and/or family for the crew. This is something to take very seriously, regardless of who comes on board as crew. As the skipper of the boat you are personally responsible for the safety of the crew and their lives, as well as your own.

Note: If you do not have Pilot charts for your planned sailing area, get some as they should be the minimum requirement for planning trips. Pilot charts provide information like the average wind speed and direction, wave and freezing on a month by month basis for a year. They are not very expensive, but many boat stores do not seem to carry them. They are available on the web at many locations. Here are a couple of sites to check out.

Government Book Store: http://bookstore.gpo.gov/subjects/sb-102.jsp

New Generation Charts:
http://www.setsail.com/store/catalog.taf?function=detail&product_id=407

From personal experience in a storm that I could have avoided, I would suggest that you should look hard at the weather every time you leave the dock. The storm that got my attention was a small one, only a 35 knot wind with 30 foot seas. The wind waves and currents changed a two hour trip into a life threatening nine hour trip. Sunnyside's bow sprint was broken; and some of the rail was ripped from the side. As they say, the pucker factor was very high for those nine hours.

Within six months I had been through a DVD training course and read a book on weather for sailors. The book and CD were less than a 1/3 of the cost of the damage to the boat. Not to speak of what could have happened.

This book will only cover a few basics of weather that should be sufficient for day sailors in small lakes. For skippers going offshore, this is another area that should receive your full attention. Take the time and find out how the weather works. Get some detailed training material or attend a course to make sure weather forecasting is a strong skill you have attained for the safety of yourself and your crew.

Basic Weather

The most valuable tool for lake sailors is the marine weather forecast that is typically available on your VHF radio. This forecast is reasonably accurate and updated frequently. If you are day sailing on a lake, at least turn on the forecast before leaving the dock to see if there is a storm coming in four hours. Taking a few minutes to find out what is forecast may result in an enjoyable and safe day for you and your crew.

The marine forecast will let you know current temperature, winds, barometer pressure and any expected changes in the weather, etc.

While at sea, if the wind is picking up and the barometer is falling, you should be listening intently to the rest of the story on the radio. That does not necessarily mean you should necessarily return to shore or for that matter not leave the dock as you can have a lot of fun in a 25 knot wind if you and your crew are ready to handle it. If everyone is not ready, do a BBQ at the dock.

The Weather

The weather is always changing. Low and high fronts keep moving around and the wind blows from high pressure toward low pressure areas trying to equalize the pressure. The sun heats the earth and causes the hot air to rise creating new low pressure zones. The air that rose cools in the atmosphere and falls back to the earth creating high pressure zones. And the wind blows.

The winds are also caused by the difference in how long it takes to heat or cool the surface of land versus water. So when the sun comes up and starts to heat the water and the land, the land heats up and the air moves up and out over the water. The air cools and falls back to the sea. This basically creates a lower pressure area on the land and a high pressure off shore. And yes, the wind blows! Maybe you have wondered in the past why the wind seems to always be blowing at the beach. Well now you know. That is how a "Sea Breeze" works.

Tools

In the chapter on communications we will cover the Weather FAX. My recommendation is similar to that of the AMEX (American Express) credit card company motto, "Don't leave home without it". If you are off shore for more than a few hours, you will need to know which way to go to try to avoid a storm. That is not obvious from verbal reports.

Storms are usually associated with a low pressure area. Low pressure areas frequently bring warm, cold, or occluded fronts with them. The fronts can make life miserable.

A low pressure area and/or storm fronts normally move at around 11-15 knots. For a power boat, you might be able to out run the storm. In a sail boat you need to do the best you can. If the storm is chasing you it will catch you unless you somehow get out of its way. Even then the waves may ripple through the ocean and make life a bit miserable for a time.

If possible, head for a high. If you get there, there may be no wind. If you are getting weather fax reports you will be able to see where the highs are located. The closer you get to the high the more distance there will be between barometric pressure zones and the wind speed should decrease accordingly.

The key to success and safety is early warning of possible weather challenges.

Another thing that I found valuable in my studies is the fact that the wind blows around a low pressure zone in a counter clockwise direction in the northern hemisphere and clockwise for a high pressure zone. (Opposite in the southern hemisphere) Take a course.

One of the ways weather conditions are reported is via use of the Beaufort Scale. I have included this for your future use below.

Beaufort Scale

Force	Knots	Description	Wave / Maximum in Feet
0	0-1	Calm	0/0
1	1-3	Light Air	.3/.3
2	4-6	Light Breeze	.7/1
3	7-10	Gentle Breeze	2/3
4	11-16	Moderate Breeze	3/5
5	17-21	Fresh Breeze	7/8
6	22-27	Strong Breeze	10/13
7	28-33	Near Gale	13/18
8	34-40	Gale	18/25
9	41-47	Severe Gale	23/33
10	48-55	Storm	30/41
11	56-63	Violent Storm	38/52
12	64+	Hurricane	46+

Chapter 19 – Emergencies

Even if you plan well there can be situations where you have an emergency or maybe just need help while you are traveling on your boat. I have had to chuckle a few times out there, but actually it is a bit sad and dangerous for the rest of us when someone beaches his or her runabout and yells Mayday.

The Coast Guard is always ready to help without calling ~~wolf~~, Mayday. If you think you need help, call the Coast Guard on your VHF radio. Ask them to meet you on Channel 22. Explain the problem and ask for some help. I have been amazed at all the help they have provided. Be careful though. The Coast Guard will typically ask for other boaters to assist. They do not normally pull you off the beach or to shore. The Coast Guard will normally call Sea Tow if someone needs assistance and if you do not have insurance it will be pricey.

Another thing you should be aware of is that if you leave your vessel unattended in the water, it may be salvaged by anyone and is no longer your vessel. While living on the East Coast there was an unethical towing guy that would come to people's rescue, ask them to come aboard his vessel, and then take ownership of the abandoned vessel. Yep, it went to court a few times, but it is the law of the sea and he won. Not too many folks appreciate buying their vessel back from a towing company.

There is a good guide line for abandoning (or just leaving) your ship. "When the boat is tied up at the dock or when the water is above your neck standing topside." Remember the big boat you are on is a lot more stable than any life raft or dingy in rough water.

If the issue at hand is in fact life threatening, you should have your life jacket on before calling the Coast Guard. Just makes a lot of sense that if you are about to sink, you should get prepared before talking on the radio. Amazingly enough, almost everyone that calls in to the Coast Guard for an emergency, never thinks to put on his or her life vest. That would not be the case on my boat. When we are offshore, we already have them on. I use the type with the CO_2 cartridge that will inflate in an emergency when a cord is manually pulled. My wife has an automatic vest that will inflate if you enter the water.

Remember "May Day" is for a life threatening event, not just to get help.

As a last resort, when off shore, the EPIRB can be initiated to signal the Coast Guard of an emergency situation. From the Coast Guard internet they have the following information on EPIRBs. http://www.uscg.mil/d11/sectorlalb/EPIRB.htm

EPIRB stands for Emergency Position Indicating Radio Beacon. When activated, it emits an emergency signal that is picked up by satellites and transmitted via land-based receivers to rescue services (i.e. the Coast Guard). There are basically two types of EPIRBs with distinct, important differences that should be considered when choosing an EPIRB.

121.5 MHz EPIRBs

On January 1, 2007, the 121.5 MHz EPIRBs are no longer to be used by boaters. This is in preparation for the February 1, 2009, when all satellite processing of distress signals from all 121.5/243 MHz beacons will terminate. If your boat came with a 121/243 MHz EPIRB, it has no value.

The new regulation applies to all Class A, B, and S 121.5/243 MHz EPIRBs, but does not impact the use of 121.5/243 MHz man overboard devices. They are designed to work directly with a base alerting unit only and not with the EPIRB satellite system.

406 MHz EPIRBs

After January 1, 2007, only the 406 MHz EPIRBs will be detected by the International Cospas-Sarsat Satellite System. This is the Satellite system which provides distress alert and location data for the search and rescue teams around the world.

Since the 406 MHz EPIRBs are digital, the search and rescue teams can retrieve information from the registration database. The information available in the database includes the beacon owner's contact information, emergency contact information, and vessel identifying characteristics. Having this information will allow the Coast Guard, or other rescue team, to respond in a timely manner with a minimal number of false alarms.

EPIRB users in the US are required (by law) to register their beacon in the 406 MHz Beacon Registration Database at: http://www.beaconregistration.noaa.gov/

You can also register by phone by calling 1-888-212-SAVE. Other users can register their beacon in their country's national beacon registration database or, if no national database is available, in the International Beacon Registration Database at https://www.406registration.com/

The 406 MHz frequency has several advantages over the 121.5 MHz frequency. Satellites store the EPIRB's position and transmit that information when it flies over a satellite receiver. This eliminates "dead zones," giving the 406 MHz EPIRB global coverage.

The stability and accuracy of the 406 MHz EPIRB signal pinpoints the EPIRB position within a 3 mile radius, allowing emergency teams to find you faster and easier.

The 406 MHz EPIRB is digital and is programmed with your vessel's ID number. When your EPIRB is activated, search & rescue teams will know who is in trouble and can attempt to get in touch with you. This cuts the false alarm rate to less than 5%.

The 406 MHz EPIRBs are available in two categories. Category I (CAT I) EPIRBs are automatically activated and released when submerged in water. Category 2 (CAT II) EPIRBs, otherwise identical to CAT I's, must be manually activated and released.

All EPIRBs are a last resort safety measure, for Mayday use only.

Another consideration for boaters is a personal EPIRB. The personal units have a GPS built in so if you are in the water, the unit can transmit an emergency signal with your correct and latest Latitude and Longitude. Having that information transmitted to the satellite will provide the rescue team a much better chance of finding you in the big ocean. The personal EPIRBs are only 406 MHz units.

Rules, Regulations, and Laws

Chapter 20 – Coast Guard Rules

All vessels must comply with federal and state requirements under penalty of law. The captain of a vessel, even a 16 foot runabout, is responsible for the safe and legal operation of the boat as well as the safety and actions of the crew.

Vessels have slightly different requirements depending on the length of the boat. The rule change points are 16', 26', 40', and 65' to 165'. I am reasonably sure that if you bought this book you fall within one of these sizes. (Unless it is a present for the new skipper you just hired.)

The best quick reference for what rules apply for each group that I have seen is a sign posted at the local West Marine in the safety equipment section of the store. It tells you at a glance what safety equipment is required for each vessel length. They also have something similar in their catalogue. The chart in the catalogue may be more useful as you can have it on your boat. (They are free too.)

On a side note there are always a lot of solutions in the West Marine catalogue that solve many problems for different types of systems. At the no cost level the catalogue is a fantastic reference book and you can even buy stuff at West Marine as well. They also provide some reasonable recommendations for different cruising scenarios, For example, Power or Sail, Inland, Coastal, or Blue Water. Since that information is readily available from a free source, it will not be replicated here. (Probably on the West Marine web site at www.westmarine.com as well as many other locations.) If you have Web access, there are many solutions posted, so look before you start. Someone probably did the task before.

Regardless of the size of your vessel, if you are going cruising there are a few things you should have on board. The "U.S. Department of Transportation – United States Coast Guard - Navigation Rules" must be kept on board. Read through it once in a while and make sure you know the basics. There are also a few other quick reference charts that are helpful in the cockpit.

Things that new boat owners often do not realize that are a part of boating are the Navigation rules. A few of the basic Navigation Rules would include.

1. If in a channel, keep to the right.
2. If you are under power, even a sail boat with the sails up, you are a power boat.
3. Basic right of way is based on who has the most capability to get out of the way. Contrary to popular belief, sailboats do not always have the right of way, even under sail. The following are vessels that even sailboats have to yield to:
   - Parked vessels.
   - Fishing vessels.
   - Vessel restricted in movement in some way.
   - Large/commercial vessels in a traffic lane (You need to stay clear by at least 100 yards).
   - Another vessel you are passing.
   - For approaching sailboats the sail boat on starboard tack.
   - A sail boat on the leeward side if on the same tack.
   - Another vessel and you are not sure what to do, give it the right of way.
4. When another vessel, usually a vessel restricted in a channel, blasts its horn five (5) times you must get out of its way. Since these are usually big vessels, they get my attention quickly.
5. Fishing in a channel where a commercial vessel would be expected to transient, such as tankers or ferry, does not provide your vessel with the right of way. Stand by for 5 blasts. Some folks also do not realize there is a $5,000 fine for sitting there, if you live through the event.
6. A rule that caught me was that vessels over 40 feet must have a trash plan. The plan must identify that you are planning to dump your trash when you get to shore. The plan must be signed and dated by the captain and all crew members.

Chapter 21 – US Coast Guard Documentation

Documentation of your boat with the US Coast Guard is something that you may want to do or in the case of cruising internationally it is a must.

The Coast Guard states that a vessel must measure at least five net tons and, with the exception of certain oil spill response vessels, must be wholly owned by a citizen of the U.S.

The basic requirements for documentation are to demonstrate ownership of the vessel, U.S. citizenship, and eligibility for the endorsement sought.

Instructions for the process may be found at:
http://www.uscg.mil/hq/cg5/nvdc/nvdcinstr.asp

To start the process the forms are located at:
http://www.uscg.mil/hq/cg5/nvdc/nvdcforms.asp

Chapter 22 – Federal Communications Commission

There are a lot of misconceptions about licensing requirements by the Federal Communications Commission (FCC) within the boating community. It usually ends up that a good and trusted friend told me so it must be true…

So you do not get into a bind, I have provided an overview to the rules.

<u>Licensing of radio equipment</u>

- I you are operating only within US waters and never communicate with vessels outside of US waters the FCC has eliminated the requirement for any license for most transmitting devices. (VHF radio, Radar, AIS, and EPIRB)

- If you travel internationally or even live near a US boarder and communicate with foreign vessels in their water, your are required to obtain a ships license and an operator permit from the FCC.

- If you install HF SSB marine radio on your boat you are required to have a ships license and operator permit. HF radio is considered to be long range communications and can, in some cases travel around the world.

- If you have a ships license you will be provided with a <u>call sign</u> for your equipment and the license will covers all the vessel transmitters. (VHF radio, Radar, AIS, and EPIRB)

- The ships license also provides a ships identification number which is commonly referred to as an MMSI. While operating in the US, you may obtain an MMSI from other sources, but when a ships license is issued, the ships identification issued by the FCC is the only number you should use in your transmitting equipment. (VHF Radio, HF Radio, EPIRB)

- If you wish to communicate on the many Amateur radio marine networks you must obtain a General or Amateur Extra Ham License.

While operating in the United States, the FCC controls the air waves, when operating outside the United States it falls under the International Telecommunications Union. In other words, the FCC's boss for international communications! Remember, in an emergency you can use and method possible, but if it is truly not an emergency, you could be held liable for illegal communications.

FCC made simple: For serious cruising on a boat or if you have an HF radio on board, you must obtain a "Ships License" and Operator Permit. You should also obtain at least a General Armature License.

Chapter 23 – State Boating Certifications

Some states are now requiring that operators of vessels receive training and/or complete a test to show some level of competence to operate the boat. Actually it just shows you at least know the rules.

In addition, even if your boat is a US Documented vessel, it may have to be registered in the state where the vessel is located. Typically this will also result in displaying a state sticker someplace on your boat as prescribed by the state. States always like to get their cut.

A personal experience I had with the testing process was in the state of Oregon and Washington. Both states have been integrating the certification requirement onto state boaters by age group over the past few years.

I took the test and was surprised. While the intent seemed to be good, there was a flaw, in my opinion, to the testing process. The test covered everything on the water with a large percentage of the questions being on personal water craft (PWC). Initially the term PWC confused me as I have never even tried a crotch-rocket-boat. I passed it, but guess which questions I missed? The ones on personal water craft. One example was that I found it amazing that they would let a jet ski pull a water skier with a person sitting backwards to watch the skier.

In Washington, they also had a lot of questions on trailers for boats. That would be nice if it actually allowed me to pull the boat, but I think even after passing the test, a trailer for a 45 foot 15 ton boat with a 52 foot mast may require a special driver's license and truck.

In my opinion there should be several certifications. The logical approach would be certifications based on the size of your vessel similar to the federal government's approach. For example, under 16', 16' – 26', 26' – 165'. The small size might include canoes, jet skis, small fishing boats, trailers, etc. The 16' – 26' would cover most of the water ski crowd, trailers with breaks, and larger fishing vessels. Above 26 feet would take care of the dedicated boaters.

It seems as though that the smaller boat drivers are usually doing something else besides boating; going fast, skiing, fishing, drinking beer etc. Opps! That was a bit negative. While they usually know a lot about those subjects, they seem to care little about boating. Boating becomes a means to the end they are trying to reach that day. Typically they are also the reason we all have to pass boating certifications.

If someone buys a 30 foot or better boat to sail in, they will probably do everything actually necessary to learn to drive it.

While some of the questions on the test may be applicable across all boating environments, above 26 feet the testing should be based around the Navigation Rules and safety at sea. It may even make sense to have a ski and fishing endorsements for boat, as they have special requirements for safety and legal operation independent of basic boating. Maybe someday they will get it right!

Bottom Line, each state has its own requirements for boats boating and operation of boats in its waters. Be sure and check them out as it might cost you a few dollars to ignore the rules. At a minimum, even if you have a federally documented vessel, you will probably have to have a state sticker. The state stickers provide revenue for the states and frequently pay for good things on the water front that make boating better. As a result I have never had an issue paying for the state fee.

Even if you have a state sticker, if you take your vessel into another state, you may be required to purchase another sticker. For example, A weekend pass for that state may be required.

One more time: Be sure and check the laws as the fines are always larger than the basic fee.

Appendix I - Calculations to buy the boat

Note: Send me an email and get a computer copy of some great computer calculations including the following boat calculations within an Excel spreadsheet to make it easy.
p-t_on_sunyside@live.com)

Show the calculation on your negotiation sheet:

➢ The average price of boats found for each following year of The Boat. Remember the lowest cost possible helps you so be sure and put some charter boats in the years closest to The Boat and <u>higher prices</u> in later models. Charters are priced lowest of all the available boats
➢ Include features provided by each boat (radar, GPS, etc) so the table will provide a reasonable evaluation of the cost.
➢ The difference in price between years For example, Price of the average 1990 – Price of the average 1989.
➢ Take the year before and after The Boat year and add or subtract the average differential price as appropriate to calculate a range of <u>reasonable prices</u> for The Boat

Example – When I bought my 1987 and list price was $130,000

1990 (Highest priced boats)

Boat A = 169,000
Boat B = 169,000
Boat C = 172,000
　　　<u>Average = $170,000</u>

1989 (Medium Priced Boats)　　　So: Difference Cost =170,000-153,900 = $16,100

Boat D = $153,900　　　Average $153,900

1988 Lowest Priced boats (Charters)

Boat E = $ 115,000   Average $122,500   So: Delta Cost = 153,900-122,500 = $31,400

Boat F = $125,000

So the range of prices for negotiation of The Boat = 1988 price – large Delta to 1988 price to smaller Delta.

Or ($122,500 – $31,400) = $91,100 to ($122,500 – $16,000) = $106,500

So the range is then $91,100 to $106,500.

Knowing that the banks love low numbers, get the NADA MAR APP Report. They really made the price look bad at **$77, 155**.

While the dealer had lots of reasons why the NADA MAR APP Report value for the boat was low, it was much harder to explain away the market list prices for comparable boats.

Be sure and look at both ends and see what makes the most sense. If the price is too ridiculous, the spread sheet will lose credibility, so pick your equivalent boats wisely and play with the spreadsheet to make sure it makes sense.

See examples on the disk provided in spreadsheet "Features_Price.xls"

Appendix II - Calculations to help select the right Boat!

Formulas for Hull Designs

- **Hull Speed Knots =** $1.34 * LWL^{0.5}$

- **Optimistic/Max Hull Speed =** $(2 * LWL)^{0.5}$

- **Displacement to length ratio =** $\dfrac{\text{Displacement}}{2240 * (0.01 \text{ X Sail Area}^3)}$

Note: Cruising starts at about <u>200.</u> Racing is <100

- **Sail Area/ Displacement Ratio =** $\dfrac{\text{Sail Area}}{\text{Displacement Ratio}^{0.666}}$

- **Where Displacement Ratio =** $\dfrac{\text{Displacement}}{64}$

Note: Mono hulls sailboats should be 6-19 and racers are much higher

- **Velocity Ratio =** $\dfrac{1.88 * LWL^{0.5} * \text{Sail Area}^{0.33}}{\text{Displacement}^{0.25} * \text{Hull Speed}}$

You are looking for anything greater than 1. The boat is under powered if less than 1.

➢ **Ballast to Displacement Ratio =** $\dfrac{\text{Ballast}}{\text{Displacement}}$

Note: Typical 0.25 to 0.5

Capsize Risk = $\dfrac{\text{Beam}}{\text{Displacement Factor}^{0.333}}$

Where Displacement factor = $\dfrac{\text{Displacement}}{0.9 * 64}$

Note: Less than 2 is Good

➢ **Comfort Factor =** $\dfrac{\text{Displacement}}{0.65 * (0.7 * \text{LWL} + (0.3 * \text{LOA})) * \text{Beam}^{1.33}}$

Note: A result of 30 to 40 is average, but the higher the number the higher the comfort rating of the boat.

Where:
LOA is the length overall.
LWL is the length waterline.
Draft is how far the boat extends below the waterline.
Beam is how wide the boat is at the widest point.
Displacement is the weight of the boat.
Ballast is the weight of the keel.
Sail Area is the total sail area including all sails that can be up at the same time.
Mast Height above waterline is, as suggested, the distance from the waterline to the top of the mast, not including antennas.
Engine HP is the Horse power of the engine.

Appendix III - NATO Phonetic Alphabet

Have this handy with your vessel and call signs to ensure good communications.

CHARACTER	MORSE CODE	TELEPHONY	PHONIC (PRONUNCIATION)
A	• —	Alfa	(AL-FAH)
B	— • • •	Bravo	(BRAH-VOH)
C	— • — •	Charlie	(CHAR-LEE) or (SHAR-LEE)
D	— • •	Delta	(DELL-TAH)
E	•	Echo	(ECK-OH)
F	• • — •	Foxtrot	(FOKS-TROT)
G	— — •	Golf	(GOLF)
H	• • • •	Hotel	(HOH-TEL)
I	• •	India	(IN-DEE-AH)
J	• — — —	Juliet	(JEW-LEE-ETT)
K	— • —	Kilo	(KEY-LOH)
L	• — • •	Lima	(LEE-MAH)
M	— —	Mike	(MIKE)
N	— •	November	(NO-VEM-BER)
O	— — —	Oscar	(OSS-CAH)
P	• — — •	Papa	(PAH-PAH)
Q	— — • —	Quebec	(KEH-BECK)
R	• — •	Romeo	(ROW-ME-OH)
S	• • •	Sierra	(SEE-AIR-RAH)
T	—	Tango	(TANG-GO)
U	• • —	Uniform	(YOU-NEE-FORM) or (OO-NEE-FORM)
V	• • • —	Victor	(VIK-TAH)
W	• — —	Whiskey	(WISS-KEY)
X	— • • —	Xray	(ECKS-RAY)
Y	— • — —	Yankee	(YANG-KEY)
Z	— — • •	Zulu	(ZOO-LOO)
1	• — — — —	One	(WUN)
2	• • — — —	Two	(TOO)
3	• • • — —	Three	(TREE)
4	• • • • —	Four	(FOW-ER)
5	• • • • •	Five	(FIFE)
6	— • • • •	Six	(SIX)
7	— — • • •	Seven	(SEV-EN)
8	— — — • •	Eight	(AIT)
9	— — — — •	Nine	(NIN-ER)
0	— — — — —	Zero	(ZEE-RO)

Sunnyside
Sierra
Uniform
November
November
Yankee
Sierra
India
Delta
Echo

AD7XL
Alpha, Delta, 7, Xray, Lima

WDA 5497
Whiskey, Delta Alpha 5497

NATO phonetic alphabet

Appendix IV – Vessel Flag Etiquette

- Stern flag: For most recreational vessels must be the flag where your vessel is documented, regardless of who is aboard or where you are located. e.g Canadian, United States, England, etc "Country" flags. It tells the Navy, Coast Guard and other countries where your vessel is from. (Errors could easily result in a boarding by officials)

- The starboard halyard is considered the side of honor and the port side is generally for working flags.

- Courtesy flags should be flown from the outermost halyard on the starboard side or if no halyard from an antenna or if your vessel is mastless, it should display the "courtesy flag" at the bow.

- You should not fly two flags from the same halyard. You may move the lesser status flag to the port side if you need to fly a second flag.

- Working flags such as "divers over the side" shall be flown from the port side.

- If you have no stern post and fly the Country flag from a center mast, it will be the highest flag on the vessel.

- Country Yacht club, Power Squadron, officer flags, and others should not be flown outside the US.

- Courtesy flags should not be flown when returning to your Country.

- When a foreign guest is aboard, you may display the ensign of the guest's country from the bow staff or outboard port spreader. Should more than one such guest flag be appropriate, wear them on spreader halyards from port to starboard in the alphabetical order of their countries' names in the English language. (Assumes multiple halyards on the port side)

For More info: http://www.usps.org/f_stuff/etiquett.html

The KISS Glossary

Aft – The back half of the boat / the middle of the boat to the non-pointy end.

Accidental Jibe – Unplanned and uncontrolled Jibe. Causes the boom for the main sail to swing from one side to the other very fast and then stop. A lot of potentially destructive energy is developed and could even dismast your boat. This is the change of course that can kill you if you are standing when the boom comes across the boat.

Ballast – Weighting of the boat in the vertical downward direction, keel / Non tip-over weight.

Beam – How wide is the boat at the widest point / the smallest distance through which your boat can squeeze.

Boat – A marine vessel less than 300 feet long / something I can afford.

Boom – Used to stretch sails out in the horizontal direction. / Also used to get rid of people who like to stand in the cockpit.

Bow – The direction the boat (hopefully) heads when under sail / the pointy end of the boat.

Brushes – In a generator the moving rotor makes electrical contact with the DC source for magnetism via contacts called brushes. The brushes are a potential failure point for generators.

Capsize Risk – A factor to provide an indication of the ability of a boat's righting moment. / Non tip-over factor

CARD – Collision Avoidance Radar Detector / Anyone else out there?

Comfort Factor – A rating that provides an indication how smoothly a vessel will ride through the water / Factor to show the wife as to how great this will be.

COG – Course Over Ground. The actual movement of the boat. Combines the boat speed with wind and currents causing the boat to move in a specific direction. What direction are we really going since it is not in the direction of the pointy end of the boat?

CPA – Closest Point of Approach. The distance another vessel will be when it comes past you. As used with your radar, you can use CPA to evaluate if you should take corrective action and do some fancy boat maneuvering.

Distance to the Horizon – The distance to the horizon is a

DSC – Digital Selective Calling   Digital message that can provide your present latitude, longitude and your (MMSI) ship's identification number in an emergency broadcast.

Draft – The distance the boat extends down into the water / how shallow can I go before the bottom keeps me from moving.

ETA – Estimated Time of Arrival. The answer for the kids on, "Are we there yet". It is the approximate time when you get there.

Forward – The front half of the boat / pointy end to the middle of the boat for most.

Galley – The kitchen on a boat / Fancy name for kitchen so not just anyone can find it.

Generator – Provides 120 VAC while away from dock / Eliminates the need for long shore power cords.

Jibe – When changing direction with the wind going across the stern of the boat as you shift from a port side wind to a starboard side wind, or vice versa.

Guesstimate – A guesstimate is also referred to as a SWAG. A Swag is defined as a scientific wild ass guess by those of us in the engineering world. That means you thought about it some before guessing.

Halyard – A rope that is used to raise the sails

Head – Toilet, Lavatory, La Banyu / A beer recycling and dumping place

Hull Speed – The fastest that a displacement hull will travel through water.

KISS – Keep It Simple Stupid. / Keep it simple stupid.

LOA – Length of boat Overall / From the pointy end to the flat end.

LWL – Length Water Line / Same as LOA, but only the part touching the water.

Mast – Used to raise sails up in the vertical direction/ Used in place of a sky hook for sails.

MHz – Million Cycles per second. Also equal to 1000 KHz where KHZ = 1000 cycles per second.

MMSI – Maritime Mobile Service Identification number. This number is assigned by the Federal Communications Commission when you obtain a station license and call sign for your vessel. If you are not getting an FCC license you may obtain an MMSI by contacting either BoatUS, Sea Tow Service International, Inc., or MariTEL.

Nautical Mile – A Nautical mile is equal to 1,852 meters (approximately 6,076 feet) or approximately 2000 yards. This is also for practical purposes the distance of a minute of Latitude.

Painter – A line that is used to tie up your dingy to the boat or pull it behind a sail boat.

Pilot Charts – Monthly charts for an area/region that provide information such as the average wind speed and direction, wave action, and freezing on a month by month basis. Pilot charts are used to plan voyages to help the skipper of a vessel keep the mast on and the top side of the boat pointing up with minimum water in the cockpit.

Port – As you face forward on the boat (pointy end for most) the left side / the side opposite the hand you put over your heart when saying the pledge of allegiance.

Rode – The line or chain you put out for the anchor line.   The rope or chain connection between the boat and the hook on the bottom.

Rope – Something you buy at the store that magically becomes a line, a painter, a halyard or a sheet when it arrives at your boat. / Used by people on shore without a sailboat or frequently for all applications on a power boat.

Sail Area – Area of all the sails on the boat used for normal sailing. On a sloop it would include the head sail and the main sail area combined./ Wind engine horsepower.

Sail and Mast Dimensions:

- I = Height of head stay termination above the sheer line
- J = Distance between the head stay termination at the deck and the front of the mast at the sheer line.
- P = Distance between black bands on the mast, or the maximum luff length of the main sail. (The luff is the front side of the sail.)
- E = Distance between black bands on the boom, or the maximum foot length of the main sail. (The foot is the lower side of the sail.)
- PY & EY are similar to P & E, but indicate mizzen mast dimensions

Sail Area Calculations

Approximate sail area calculations.

- Mainsail Area = P x E / 2
- Headsail Area = (Luff x LP) / 2
  (LP is the shortest distance between the clew and the luff)
- Approx. 150% Genoa Area = (1.5 x J x I) / 2
- Approx. 135% Genoa Area = (1.35 x J x I) / 2
- 100% Fore triangle = (I x J) / 2
- Approx. Spinnaker Area = 1.8 x J x I

Salon – The living room on a boat. / Area where wine and beer are consumed in port.

Sea Breeze – When the sun heats the land and water at different rates causing the air to rise over the land, cool, and fall onto the ocean increasing the pressure and blowing back to the shore. (When the heated air over the land rises, cooler air from the ocean flows toward land to replace the rising air.)

Sheet – A line that is used to control the position of a sail. / Not associated with a state room.

SOG – Speed Over Ground. How fast are we really going? Like Course Over Ground (COG) the SOG takes into account the wind and currents pushing the boat in their directions. If we are headed into a current of 3 knots and our boat speed is 3 knots, on the earth we are standing still. If the current goes away, we are traveling up river at 3 knots. SOG would be 0 and 3 respectively.

Starboard - As you face forward on the boat (pointy end for most) the Right side of the boat / the hand you put over your heart when saying the pledge of allegiance.

State Room – Bed room on a boat / Where the action happens.

Stern – As you face forward on the boat (pointy end for most) it is behind you / the non pointy end for most boats.

Tack – When changing direction with the wind going across the bow of the boat as you shift from a port side wind to a starboard side wind or starboard side to port.

Vang – Holds the boom down on a run / Something to look at when steering the boat.

Wavelength – In meters = 300/the frequency in MHz   MHz = 1000 KHz

Yacht – A marine vessel that is greater than 50 feet long / a boat that uses china to eat on and is typically owned by someone else.

Made in the USA
Charleston, SC
10 July 2011